SPECULATIVE INSTRUMENTS

Speculative Instruments

by

I. A. RICHARDS

THE UNIVERSITY OF CHICAGO PRESS

CHICAGO · ILLINOIS

THE UNIVERSITY OF CHICAGO PRESS · CHICAGO 37
Routledge & Kegan Paul, Ltd., London, E.C.4
The University of Toronto Press, Toronto 5, Canada

CONTENTS

For if anything in the world is desirable, so desirable that even the dull and brutish herd would, in its more reflective moments, prize it above silver and gold, it is that a ray of light should fall on the darkness of our being, and that we should come by some explanation of our mysterious existence where nothing is clear but its wretchedness and futility. But even if this were attainable in itself, it is made impossible by the compulsory solutions that are forced upon us.

SCHOPENHAUER

Keep the Will one.
Do not listen with the Ear rather than the Mind;
Do not listen with the Mind rather than the Spirit.
The work of the Ear ends with hearing;
The work of the Mind ends with ideas.
But the Spirit is an emptiness ready to take in all
    Things.
Tao abides in the emptiness
The emptiness is The Fast of the Mind.

CHUANG TZU

FOREWORD

THESE pieces were composed at different times and for very different occasions and audiences. They were articles, formal lectures, addresses, notes for talks. What brings them together into, I believe, a considerable unity is their common concern with interpretation, with the politics of the divided mind and with the resolutions which generate intelligibility and comprehension. They return again and again to certain common purposes, endeavouring to present and explore them for audiences of widely varying resources and preparation. And since these purposes, for the most part, are such that no one knows what preparation would be best or how we should equip ourselves to pursue them, there is an advantage in thus bringing together a variety of attempts at treatment. Furthermore, there are those, with whom I count myself, who find more interest in reading what was written for others.

One man's light is another man's darkness; and these purposes (my reader will see why I do not yet precisely name them), beyond all others perhaps, invite us to mix the absurd with the profound, indeed to transmute them. The very same sentences may be either or both, as the other sentences they are taken with are changed. Interpretation: taking together with. And the other sentences do not need to be formulated or uttered: they can be operative without that. Remarks on these themes have therefore a perennial alibi as well as a daunting exposure. They may seem—even be—wild vagaries; on the other hand they could score inners at least. For shifts in the other sentences within which they are interpreted also shift the target.

These remarks here in this Foreword, like those they are about, suffer and enjoy to the full all these penalties and immunities, for they are not merely discourse on discourse, but discourse on that. How is discourse possible and whence do its perils and frustrations arise? Which sorts of discourse may most be trusted? No great *quantity* of experience is needed to enable us to discern that discourse on discourse must be as untrustworthy as any— which last remark was ⁴discourse⁴ and turned, after the dash, to ⁵discourse⁵ and ⁶discourse⁶.

The most central theme of these attempts may be the recognition that most ways of studying language use language and must expect to take the consequences. None of these pieces hopes to *say* what these consequences may be. The medium, the instrument through which we *say*, is not so simple as such a hope would imply. However, and this is their sounder hope, familiarity with tricky, if not treacherous, situations can work wonders—as the diplomat and the cragsman can show. It is the aim of this collection of essays to increase—for those who have a taste for such hazardous ground—to increase familiarity with situations in which we are trying to see what is being said and trying to separate it from what is not being said, situations above all in which we would, if we could, investigate our intellective instruments themselves, the tools with which we work in all investigation.

The order in which I have placed my attempts may gain from a short explanation. In the first piece I play with the suggestion that the present role of philosophy should be that of a Diplomacy attempting some mitigation of the conflicts between the opposing studies. Any reader who likes to reverse it also and make it into a plea for a more enterprising and venturesome diplomacy between the nations will not be misreading. Many of the great metaphors are reversibles. Piece II, 'Toward a Theory of Comprehension', may, I fancy, be the most positive and stable thing in the volume: a provisional setting up of a schema to aid comparisons between the 'Total Meanings' of utterances. If thought is comparing (paralleling in one respect or another), in what respects may meanings be most usefully compared? The diagram which results will serve, I hope, as support and control to the following pieces which are more elliptic, more superficial, more popular. As an attempt to present a comprehensive view of comprehending, Piece II does not profess to be itself exceptionally comprehensible; and the reader who does not find it so may be very well advised to pass by—for the time being—either to III or IV. III, 'Emotive Meaning Again', is addressed in the first place to readers who may have met remarks of mine in this topic penned some time ago; but it moves on from this *liaison* work to discuss what we need such a 'speculative instrument' as is sketched in II for, and the dependent query: 'What sort of an instrument therefore should it be?' And it amplifies the *Universal Studies : United Nations* parallel already referred to in this Foreword.

Piece IV, 'The Future of the Humanities', opens up the pedagogic concern of these studies. No one, I imagine, migrates from Literature to Education for fun, but through a feeling as to what will happen if we do not develop improved teaching soon enough. The Comics and the other Mass Media are on the Rampage and remedies must be sought.

Piece V, 'Education and Culture', follows this up and VII reconnects this interest in teaching to the central theme: not doctrine but discernment—the concern of II and III. The ensuing pieces point this moral for various audiences and at different levels. VIII develops a suggestion that 'What should come before what?' may be the query which most matters to the design of better teaching.

With IX, 'The Idea of a University', we climb up again from the seed beds to consider the ecology of the Garden Plato founded: rivalries between faculties—in the Academy or in the Mind. And with X we are back again where Piece I and Piece II left us.

Section Two consists of six pieces addressed originally to audiences with some special interest or faculty orientation: five informal talks and one review. I have kept the informality, for the most part, believing that academic writing today is too often overdressed: out of accord with the fugacious character of what it has to say. Moreover the concern of these pieces is with the questions they may awake rather than with any answers they could impart. I hope they are care-free without being careless in manner.

Section Three contains two pieces: one illustrating the difficulties of reading; the other the underground of tradition to which the greatest writers seem to have access. Their greatness is that they can make us share it.

I. A. R.

Srinagar, Kashmir
December, 1954

Grateful acknowledgments are due for permission to reprint to the Editors of the following periodicals where these Pieces first appeared: *Confluence* (I), *The Philosophical Review* (III), *The Journal of General Education* (IV), *The Partisan Review* (V), *Furioso* (VI), *The Yale Review* (VII), *The Kenyon Review* (XV), *The Criterion* (XVII), *The Hudson Review* (XVIII).

Section One

I

Notes toward an Agreement between Literary Criticism and Some of the Sciences

IT is not as yet very clear which of the Studies—to use a comprehensive name—are invited to consider becoming signatories to the proposed Agreement. That will depend upon the terms which finally appear in the Agreement and upon how far, and to which of the Studies, they are intelligible. It will also depend upon which of the Studies have developed examinable purposes and appropriate accounts of their purposes and their methodologies. At this stage, however, it is enough that certain Studies should be ready to come forward—though in an unofficial and self-appointed capacity—to represent some of the major powerblocks (*a somewhat negative designation!*) among the Studies and consider jointly whether some sort of Agreement may be possible.

May, *may*, indeed, be the first and the last word in any such approaches—if it may!

The writer of these notes is aware behind his pen of two voices—indeed of many more than two, but two speak (to him, in him and through him) with more assurance and would-be authority than the rest. He has to suppose that his readers have a somewhat similar diversity of voices available with which to read what he writes. These voices do not speak at all

3

times with equal confidence and clarity. While some Sciences have the floor, Literary Criticism (which is always rather amused by its title) listens confused, inarticulate, and aghast. And some Sciences, in their turn, suffer the embarrassments of adults unaccustomed to children when Literary Criticism pipes up in its play! However, they co-exist and in the hope that their co-existence may thereby gain some mutual easements (in the general and the legal senses) they now attempt a draft of something they might jointly sign. The writer accordingly regards himself only as a Secretary—somewhat embarrassed to be simultaneously at the command of such sovereign contenders. His compensation or revenge is that he can add observations (in italics) upon a variety of points, including their sometimes imperious handling of those long-suffering servants : our words. Each of his Masters has repeatedly enjoined upon him that these Notes can at best be jottings for a hypothetical aide-mémoire *which might be glanced at in considering what might be touched on in some very tentative rough draft. None the less every other word becomes a battleground :* 'approaches', *for example, above, has replaced* 'inquiries'—*the dignity of several of the approachers having been sparked by an injudicious question :* 'Who is to do the inquiring?' *It becomes clearer at every step that this is a* diplomatic *effort. What a comedown for Philosophy! However* . . .

Within such 'may . . . may' brackets (*which are dually permissive and probabilist*) we may use what will look like straight indicatives. We may seem to make assertions, to lay out statements in arguments as though they were ironfast links in a chain and to unfold conclusions from what will formally appear to be premises. But our 'may . . . may' brackets may remind us that any meaning any word may have floats upon a primitive raft of consents. It can mean what it may only for those who will let it. An argumentative link—in a similar fashion—depends upon the structure of the meanings its interpreters will allow to be operative. And a conclusion, no less frequently here than

4

elsewhere, is of interest chiefly through what it may bring out about its premises. These assertions, arguments and developments, therefore, are no journey we take from established starting points (*which could only be established by agreement, and agreement on such things is precisely what we hope to approach*): they are manœuvres designed to increase both the probability of consents to mean in certain ways and the probability that the invitations anyone accepts will be those extended to him.

In brief, the aim of this bracketing is to increase the recognition of mutual dependence among the meanings consorting within it. The enclosed efforts can be justified only within this encompassing strategic frame and their justification will be in making the enclosing overall frame of purpose (within which they have to live together) more apparent and more acceptable to them all.

This situation may be found in a myriad forms on every scale: from the internal economy of the cell on up through the organs to the organism and out beyond in every group and association, every political structure, every culture, until it appears in its fullest richness in the endeavours of the United Nations and their analogue, the Universal Studies (*though of course for 'apparent' and 'acceptable to' we have to substitute 'sensitive' and 'co-operative with' as we go down and as we go up in scale from the normal individual man*). The situation may be further illustrated from fields as diverse as the words in a language, the *vélléities* in a mood and the changes in the weather. There is a control which seems to be exerted by a government over the possibilities of what it rules but this may equally be considered as a mutual control of the governed exerted through their government.

This way of describing the paradox of Unity is Plato's; it is an extrapolation from the mind-city analogy of *The Republic*. It substitutes for 'interests within the state' 'subjects (or components) within the culture'. But Plato (in spite of Socrates) rested in the dream of a civil service which those who do not identify themselves with it for the most part detest; Logic, Grammar, and Rhetoric have been the parallel civil service—the executives and police—among the component subjects, and have been found equally detestable. Our task could be sketched by asking: How arrange for the citizen subjects to rule one another without the intervention of these sheep-dog lovers of honour? Plato tried to cure strife by giving a special education to a chosen few. Must we be more ambitious and attempt a universal education for all? And what could that be but an outcome—only abstractly conceivable at present —of the mutual education of the subjects?

Toward that our hoped-for Agreement will be aimed.

As usual it is less the finished document than the steps toward it which are instructive, for under these steps the skeletons of the scandals lie buried—the desperate last-minute uncertainties, the fevered consultations of subordinates as to a view to recommend on the most obvious matters, the improvisations and inspirations, the vacillations and tergiversations of the experts, the withdrawal symptoms and techniques and much else. It is these which should be displayed as fully as decency permits . . . but there are intellectual cupboards no scholar, at least, will wish to see opened.

Not much difficulty is anticipated over what have come to be known as the *culpa* clauses, over *the signing* of them, that is; their observance, it is recognized, may be entirely another matter. For they concern a distinction on which the Parties will by no means see eye to eye—the distinction between truthful description and abuse, between factual and evaluative language. What one man regards as a plain statement, may seem to another an outrageous calumny—and whether the phrase 'outrageous calumny' (truly or falsely applied) is itself factual or evaluative affords in its turn an opportunity for dispute. Indeed these *culpa* clauses (which follow) are foreseen by some to be

6

likely (though their intention is most commendable) to make the conflicts harder rather than easier to extinguish. Rules are more easily agreed upon than the choice of the instances to be placed under them. However, here they are.

The High Contracting Parties hereby endeavour to agree:

1. That none of them has or can have any clear, precise, or consistent view of any of the others.

2. That what information each possesses about the others is based on hearsay reports which have undergone incalculable transformations through intellectual translation.

3. That intermediaries are to be suspected of distorting their reports through self-interest: since they are for the most part agents employed by the Studies—sometimes by several at once—and are naturally anxious to please their employers.

4. That the overall philosophies hitherto developed to prevent or ease conflicts between the Studies have been associations concerned to promote the interests of one party or another among the Studies and have thus tended rather to increase than to diminish tension and suspicion.

5. That courtesy, decorum, and good manners are a chief means whereby improved relations between the Studies may be forwarded and that abusive language used in complaints is an indication that the guilt is not wholly where it is alleged to be.

6. That complaints be drawn up—so far as is possible —in *neutral* language. It is recognized that *neutral* here is a term in need of a clarification—toward which the following schedules of grievances and complaints are offered. It will be evident that expressions occur in this exhibit whose use may be regarded as a breach of this clause.

I

Complaints brought by Literary Criticism against other Studies—principally against some describing themselves as Sciences.

A. That a Study widely known of late as Linguistic Science has in the important matter of *choice of words* attempted to usurp authority long recognized to belong inalienably to Literary Criticism. This unwarrantable and aggressive behaviour is defended on the ground that how men actually do speak and write is sufficient to determine how men *should* speak and write, that factual evidence of usage is decisive, and that in the face of properly authenticated records of men's customs in the use of words the preferences of literary critics are irrelevant and their findings inadmissible.

It will be noted that the word should *recurs as chief bone of contention for some of the other complaints which follow. There is a struggle in process for the control of this key strategic point and these complaints together with their counter complaints are evidence for differing concepts of what may be needed to command it. Or perhaps the contention is between a set of concepts—a relatively powerless long-range vision or prehension of the good order—and an exploratory technique of bulldozing power unprovided with distance receptors.*

Literary Criticism's complaint continues: The recommendation that we should follow *and teach* majority usage just because it is majority usage, and without regard for qualified judgment as to which usages are to be preferred to which and for what reasons, constitutes a destructive invasion of the Humanities by an as yet methodologically uninstructed and philosophically ignorant branch, or satellite, of Science. It should be added that nothing in this description should be construed as derogatory to Linguistic Science as operating within its proper field.

8

Recent advances of descriptive linguistics are among the glories of our time, as surprising and alarming as those in medicine, physics, or logic. But the proper field of descriptive linguistics does not include any territory of the Humanities or of Literary Criticism or of the pedagogy for which they are responsible.

The judgment as to which expressions are preferable to which—when, for what, and why—belongs to the Humanities in the sense in which Shakespeare is their true proficient. No doubt the Humanities at times—absorbed in palace pleasures and past glories—have neglected their frontiers; but that does not license other studies to attempt what only the Humanities can do. Only the mind which has been concerned with and trained in the Humanities knows how hard it is to decide which of a number of phrases will be best for what we may call a given meaning, and how much that depends upon what other phrases are in relevant relation to it. The humanist is experienced in such choices, in the discernment of relevancies. Through this experience he has learned how to respect the language. The Linguistic Scientist whose aggressions are here complained of does not know how to respect the language. He does not yet have a conception of the language which would make it respectable. He thinks of it as a *code* and has not yet learned that it is an organ—the supreme organ of the mind's self-ordering growth. Despite all his claims to be expert in collecting, reporting, comparing, and systematizing linguistic facts, he has not yet apprehended the greatest of them all: that language is an instrument for controlling our becoming.

A sentence we speak or write—like any other line of behaviour—will realize some possibilities and fail to realize others. Values come in with our choices as to which possibilities are to be (*should be*) realized. If the possibilities to be realized are such and such, then a certain phrasing will be best. But note well the *if* here. Linguistic

9

science can and will help us to see which phrasings will do what, but it cannot, *as science*, settle which possibilities are *to be realized*. As students of the humanities, we know this to be a deeper matter than any science, as yet, has explored; a matter of what man is and should be, of what his world is and should be, of what the God he should worship and obey is and should be. All this, the Scientist —linguistic or other—will admit to be beyond his purview *as a Scientist*. What is done and what can be done he can inquire into, but what should be done is not within his province.

If this invasion is not repelled two great and not easily corrigible evils follow: a conformity-minded speech community—the dream-public of the advertiser and the politico—and a degradation of the language. Of this last, two instances may be given, familiar and well worn—as they should be.

1. More people seem to be saying *disinterested* when they should mean *uninterested*: 'The class was completely disinterested in what the teacher was doing.' If the Linguistic Scientist found the whole world writing and speaking so, that would only mean that a noble distinction, hard to replace, had been lost.

2. Uses of *imply* and *infer* are, it is true, regional; and it is true that Milton uses *infer* where the best current use would be *imply*. It is the best use because it allows us— better than in any other way—to make distinctions we need to make, as follows:

Given some utterance, a person may infer from it all sorts of things which neither the utterance nor the utterer implied. And further, an utterer may imply things which his hearers cannot reasonably infer from what he says. In short the best current uses of the two words handle with beautiful efficiency an endlessly recurrent set of problems which attend the word *say*: the disaccords between sayer and sayee as to just how much has been said. Wherever *imply* and *infer* are used indifferently or confusedly a valuable power is forgone. And, once again, though all the world forwent it, that would no more show its loss to be good, than a general habit of promiscuity would show that to be good.

B. That a group of Studies led by History has been and is endeavouring by underground tactics to invert the covenants of the trust held by Literary Criticism. The activities directed to this end amount to psychological warfare of which the following may serve as type specimen:

> Any book, any essay, any note in *Notes and Queries*, which produces a fact even of the lowest order about a work of art is a better piece of work than nine-tenths of the most pretentious critical journalism, in journals or in books.

What critic faced by this can feel sure that he too is not a most pretentious journalist? Is it surprising if he takes to biography or literary history, however queer the notion of 'fact' may often be in these fields?

These attempts to seduce literary critics and destroy their allegiance are none the better for being practised on the side by men of letters, sometimes eminent. The type specimen above is from an august pen. And this Fifth Columnist infiltration is still less tolerable in that a widespread conspiracy exists to overthrow government and seize power in Literary Criticism and its allied Studies and to transform them into merely factual administrations on the model of sundry Sciences commonly known as Social. Agents employed in this conspiracy are to be found in high positions. How far they are aware of what they are doing, how far they are dupes, and how far they are merely following a fashion are questions which remain to be determined.

C. That a group of Studies which has in the last fifty years seized the title and territory of Psychology is now intent upon extending its conquests from this heartland

11

into the few, the terribly undefended and last remaining strongholds of free will. As we would expect, this conscienceless—and indeed consciousness-stripped—assault is excused as being a necessary measure of defence on the part of the heartland, a reaction to age-long and insufferable interference in its internal affairs, and to continued obstruction and frustration of its growth and development. As a type specimen the following may be entered:

> Science is not just concerned with 'getting the facts' after which one may act with greater wisdom in an unscientific fashion. Science supplies its own wisdom. . . . We cannot apply the methods of science to a subject matter which is assumed to move capriciously about. Science not only describes, it predicts. It deals not only with the past but with the future. Nor is prediction the last word: to the extent that relevant conditions can be . . . controlled, the future can be controlled. If we are to use the methods of science in the field of human affairs, we must assume that behavior is lawful and determined. This possibility is offensive to many people. . . . It is opposed to a tradition of long standing which regards man as a free agent whose behavior is the product, not of specifiable antecedent conditions, but of spontaneous inner changes. . . .
>
> A scientific conception of human behavior dictates one practice, a philosophy of personal freedom another. . . . We shall almost certainly remain ineffective in the field of human affairs until we adopt a consistent point of view and develop a consistent code of action.

Accordingly, the proper development of this mode of controlling the future requires the dislodgement of 'a philosophy of personal freedom' now uncovered as the prime preventive of a happier world. Literary criticism, as the guardian Study most widely responsible for maintaining the art of choice—that exercise of personal freedom—protests in the name of all the humanities against this attempted usurpation.

D. A somewhat similar complaint is in preparation against Anthropology as aiming to reshape the definition of *culture* and thereby reduce Literary Criticism to the role of apologist for the passing fashion.

II

Complaints brought by the Sciences against Literary Criticism.

It is regrettable that a certain dilatoriness in preparing their charges on the part of the Sciences has to be remarked. They would almost seem to have not as yet given the matter the attention it deserves. Apart from some pronouncements similar to those quoted in Literary Criticism's Complaint C, above, and sundry disdainful references to mentalism and teleology, few current formulations can be found, such as there are being hardly more than echoes of Peacock's regret that poetry should still beguile good minds:

It is a lamentable thing to see minds, capable of better things, running to seed in the specious indolence of these empty aimless mockeries of intellectual exertion. . . . Poetry was the mental rattle that awakened the attention of intellect in the infancy of civil society: but for the maturity of mind to make a serious business of the playthings of its childhood, is as absurd as for a full-grown man to rub his gums with coral, and cry to be charmed asleep by the jingle of silver bells . . .

This danger, however, appears to the Sciences to be diminishing—a view supported by Economics which has striking figures at hand as to the wages which today reward literary and scientific qualifications outside the teaching profession. The startling scarcity of scientifically qualified persons inside that profession is also sadly indicative. Indeed in the notion that the Sciences have complaints against Literary Criticism there is something oddly reminiscent of Achilles' words to Hector:

How can wolves and lambs be friends? They must hate one another for ever!

Poor wolves to have suffered so from the implacable lambs!

While awaiting the detail of their complaints, it may be wise to sketch in suitably provisional outline some considerations by which such tensions may conceivably be reduced.

It appears that a central representative issue over which conflict arises is free will versus determination and on this it seems possibly promising to suggest anew that no formulation of this opposition jointly acceptable to both sides has as yet been attained despite endless labour (and the best efforts of Milton's newly fallen fiends) devoted to just that formulation. We are back, it will be observed, at the first of the *culpa* clauses, which seeks to have the ignorance in which the Parties stand as to one another's real positions publicly recognized. While this ignorance continues, it may well be that the doctrines, the aims, the endeavours that one Party is actually attached to and operating through (as distinct from those openly professed and propagandized) may not be in such flagrant conflict as is supposed with those of the other. Their heroic confidence that this or that point of principle is one over which there can be no give and take, no negotiation, may be somewhat out of place. The history of culture is full of clashes which seemed at their height to be ultimate and unreconcilable. A little later a choice of middle ways, of other decisions, replaced them. So it may be here in this Free Will *v.* Control opposition. Actions, we all know, speak louder than words; but actions have a way of sounding strangely different through different loudspeakers and the passage of time, the shifting situation, acts like a varying microphone—stressing some aspects and diminishing others. Are there really reasons to be sure that 'A scientific conception of human behaviour dictates one practice, a philosophy of personal freedom another'? And would these reasons belong to Experimental Psychology (*in its present stage*) or to something else for which Experimental Psychology (*in its present stage*) has no authority to speak? What warrant has Experimental Psychology (*as yet*) to decide what 'a philosophy of personal freedom' dictates? (*Such a philosophy would seem to be deprived by constitution of the dictator's powers.*) These certainties seem to have a far from scientific source: they belong to what an earlier Psychology might have called 'The Revolutionary Spirit'. Furthermore, what conception of caprice—of the will at its most willful—can a strictly deterministic Psychology form? The Free-willists and the Determinists alike deprive themselves formally of the possibility of conceiving one another's key assumptions: a situation which has long been recognized and long been the delight of the short story writer and dramatist and of the Literary Critic.

None the less it is easy for all to see why the experimentalist has to assume that the behaviour he studies is 'lawful' (*an awful instance, this use of this word, of literary legerdemain*). He might as well shut up his laboratory and feast on pigeon pie, if it were not. He uses his experimentalist's skill to make that behaviour lawful in his experimentalist's meaning of that word. But that meaning is a very long way from being a meaning which a philosophy of personal freedom which knows its business is concerned to dispute. There enters here a quantitative consideration. The degree of complexity, the number and variety of the components and the multiplicity and specialty of interdependences operative in the poets the Literary Critic studies, is so much higher than in the Experimentalist's pigeons, clever birds though they be, that 'lawful' changes meaning in the vast ascent. It reassumes many of the ethical and legal implications the Experimentalist stripped from it. 'Poets are the legislators of the world', as Shelley very justly replied to Peacock.

In claiming for this sort of behaviour—operant behaviour guided by the widest and most delicate assessment of relevancies—a character for which 'freedom' is a convenient name, the Literary Critic need not be in the least disposed to deny that some of his other behaviour is as much 'the product of specifiable antecedent conditions' as the Experimentalist could wish. And these conditions may even be such that the Experimentalist could specify them. 'Specifiable' is the strife-breeder here. It may mean 'theoretically specifiable' (i.e. specifiable by God), in which case we have the doctrine of freedom expounded in *Paradise Lost*. Or it may mean 'able to be specified by some conceivable human Experimentalist.' The Literary Critic may well be content to follow Milton, but to dismiss the human Experimentalist as being definitely 'above himself' in such pretensions. The Critic knows too much about the multiplicity and interrelatedness of the independent variables to be impressed by such simplifications. After all, relevancies are his lifelong study. He may indeed be willing to agree that a theoretical determinism which leaves the specifying of the antecedents to God may be what he calls 'freedom'. He has seen it called 'perfect freedom'. But he remembers that man falls from this ideal, neglecting relevancies. And even further, he may be willing to agree that, if the account could be encompassing enough, fact would determine value. What he *should* choose would be settled by what he is responsive to. This is, after all, the founding doctrine of his profession—the Platonic 'Knowledge is virtue, virtue Knowledge.' But the account never is encompassing enough.

This instance of a source of mutual misunderstanding and tension between Studies may be generalized. The hierarchy of the complexities merits more attention than it receives. Systems of higher complexity can exercise a control over themselves which less complex systems cannot. The less complex may be subject to laws which the more complex can abrogate. So at innumerable points of inco-ordination between the studies, more attention to the degree of complexity of the occurrences under study and its outcome in the types of instrument and concept required, might smooth some of these discontinuities out.

But there is already in these Notes more than Literary Criticism itself may be expected to agree upon, let alone other Studies.

II

Toward a Theory of Comprehending[1]

LOOKING back, across more than a score of years, on the considerations with which *Mencius on the Mind* was concerned, it seems to me now that the togethernesses, the mutualities, of those considerations were omitted. There were distinctions made and differences stressed between sorts of meaning, but why they should be so made and so stressed hardly became apparent. The last chapter, 'Towards a Technique for Comparative Studies', was suitably tentative in title and in treatment. It stammered away persistently, but what it was trying to say never, *as a whole*, got said. I have some doubts whether any whole was in any steady way in the mind of the sayer. The book was written hurriedly, in a whirl of lecturing on *Ulysses* and on *The Possessed*, during a first teaching visit to Harvard. It was worked up from notes made between Tsing Hua and Yenching, under the guidance of divers advisers, and written out with much of the feeling one has in trying to scribble down a dream before it fades away. The intellectual currencies of the Harvard scene, not to mention Leopold Bloom and Stavrogin, were driving out those Chinese *aperçus* all the while. Then the only manuscript was lost, stolen by Li An-che's cook by

[1] This Essay appeared, under the title "Towards a Theory of Translating" in *Studies in Chinese Thought*, edited by Arthur F. Wright, 1953, Chicago, University of Chicago Press, to whom I am indebted for permission to reprint it here.

mistake. It lay on a house roof for some months, tossed there by the thief the instant he perceived how worthless it was. Then odd pages began blowing up and down the *hutung*; rumour spread and a search was made; it was found and returned to me—just in time to be compared with the proofs of a second version I had been recollecting back home again in Cambridge, where yet another local logical game had been offering yet other guide lines to be avoided. All useful experience, no doubt, in guessing about *what* makes *what* seem to mean *what*—*when*, *where*, and to *whom*—but not then and there conducive to a single comprehensive view of comprehending.

This, I now suppose, is what one should attempt to form. I suppose too that a first condition of the endeavour is a recognition of its inherent wilfulness. It is purposive; it seeks. If asked *what* it seeks, its only just answer should be: 'Itself'. It seeks to comprehend what comprehending may be. What is sought is the search.

Yet it advances. When it looks back upon its earlier phases, what it most notes are the things it took for granted *without* having put its requests into any but most indefinite form. It can bring the request and the grant nearer to terms for ever without any fear of arriving. The process of refining its assumptions must be just as endless as the endeavour itself.

Through these assumptions it divides and combines[1]— dividing in order to combine, combining in order to divide—and simultaneously. Whatever it compares is compared in a respect or in respects. These respects are the instruments of the exploration. And it is with them as with the instruments of investigation in physics but more so: the properties of the instruments enter into the account of the investigation. There is thus at the heart of any

[1] *Phaedrus*, 265D–266B. I have written further on 'these processes of division and bringing together' in *How To Read a Page* (London: Routledge & Kegan Paul, 1943), pp. 217–22.

theory of meanings a principle of the instrument. The exploration of comprehension is the task of devising a system of instruments for comparing meanings. But these systems, these instruments, are themselves comparable. They belong with what they compare and are subject in the end to one another. Indeed, this mutual subjection or control seems to be the ἀρχή for a doctrine of comprehension—that upon which all else depends.[1]

There is a seeming opposition to be reconciled here. We may suppose there to be a hierarchy of instruments, each caring for those below and cared for by those above. Or we may suppose the system to be circular. I have leaned here toward a position somewhat like that of the constitutional monarchist who supports an authority which is itself under control (see Aspect **6** below). The same question seems to me to appear again as: 'How should we structure the most embracing purpose?' and this I take to be an invitation to an inquiry into Justice on Platonic lines.

This mutual control shows itself in any segment of activity (any stretch of discourse, for example) as accordance and discordance of means with ends. Ends endeavour to choose means which will choose them. The entirety of activity, if, obeying Aristotle, we may venture to attempt to conceive it, seems to consist of *choices*. Initial choices would be free; but, when choice has been made, the subsequent choices are bound thereby while the choice is held. An interpretation knows only a part, often a very small part, of the entailments of its choices. These entailments may later seem to it to be 'brute fact'—something in no way and in no measure due to its choices, something upon which their success or failure depends. This is the defectiveness of the choices—made too soon or not made when choice was needed.

Enough of these preliminaries. They seemed necessary to the introduction here of the word LET as the first and

[1] *Republic*, 511C. See *How To Read a Page*, Index: 'Dependence'.

19

all-important move in this undertaking. Let *let* rule every meaning for every word in every sentence which follows. These sentences will seem for the most part to be in the indicative, but that is for brevity and for custom's sake. Everything which seems to be said in the indicative floats on a raft of optative invitations to mean in such wise. Any theory of meanings which can serve as authority, as more embracing purpose, to a theory of translation is concerned with the mutual tension of whatever can be put together to serve as that raft.

Such are among the reflections which translation between diverse cultures can occasion. How may we compare what a sentence in English may mean with what a sentence in Chinese may mean? The only sound traditional answer is in terms of two scholarships—one in English, the other in Chinese. But a scepticism which can be liberating rather than paralysing may make us doubtful of the sufficiency of our techniques for comparing meanings even within one tradition. How can one compare a sentence in English poetry with one (however like it) in English prose? Or indeed any two sentences, or the same sentence, in different settings? What is synonymy?[1] A proliferous literature of critical and interpretative theory witnesses to the difficulty. It seems to have been felt more and more in recent decades. Is there any reason to doubt that analogous difficulties await analogous efforts for Chinese? They may well have been attending the conduct of that language all along.

These troubles come, perhaps, in part from insufficient attention to the comparing activity itself. How do we compare other things? Let us see whether what we do in comparing boxes or rooms can be helpful in suggesting what we might do in comparing meanings. What would a sort of geometry of comprehendings be like? With

[1] See, e.g., Willard V. O. Quine, 'Two Dogmas of Empiricism', *Philosophical Review*, Vol. LX (1951).

rooms, we need, in the simplest cases, three dimensions. With length, breadth, and height ascertained, we have gone some way toward discovering how far one room is like another. Would it be useful to ask in how many 'dimensions' meanings may agree or differ? It might be wise to drop the geometric word and generalize at once. Let us say, then, 'in how many respects'—remembering that meanings may, if we so wish, be compared in an indefinitely great number of respects or in as few as will serve some purpose. The purpose decides which respects are relevant. This is true of rooms, too. So our problem is one of choice. What is the simplest system of respects which would enable us to compare meanings in a way serviceable to the translator's purposes? (As three dimensions serve us in comparing sizes and shapes.)

I have just called this a *problem*. If a problem is something which has a solution, I should not have done so. In my opening sentence I called such things *considerations*, hoping thereby to suggest that they are fields of unlimited speculation—held within only the most unlimited framework that even sidereal space could symbolize—and not, as problems in a branch of mathematics may be, formed and given their solutions by the assumptions which set them up. What this theory of meaning should be or do is not in this narrow sense a problem.

It is, on the other hand, the most searching of all considerations, for it is concerned with arranging our techniques for arranging. Since the system of respects is set up to serve our comparings, the respects in it must not be too many or too few, and they will probably vary with the comparing. But this cannot itself be described except by means of the respects which serve it, being the comparing which these respects implement and enable. (Similarly, the comparing of sizes and shapes cannot be described except by reference to the spatial dimensions.) In brief, we make an instrument and try it out. Only by trying it out can we discover what it can do for us. Likewise, only such trial can develop our comprehending of what it is with which we seek to explore comprehending. Thus what ensues will be a depiction of the whereby and the wherefore as well as the what.

We may begin by adapting the conventional diagram of the communication engineer to our wider purposes.[1] In translation we have two such diagrams to consider as a minimum. There will be (say) a Chinese communication for which we find ourselves in the role of Destination; and we assume thereupon the role of Sources for a communication in English. But since other communications in

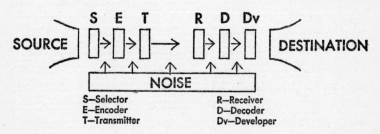

<table>
<tr><td>S—Selector</td><td>R—Receiver</td></tr>
<tr><td>E—Encoder</td><td>D—Decoder</td></tr>
<tr><td>T—Transmitter</td><td>Dv—Developer</td></tr>
</table>

Chinese and other communications in English, having *something in common* with the present communication, come in to guide the encodings and decodings, the process becomes very complex. We have here indeed what may very probably be the most complex type of event yet produced in the evolution of the cosmos.

Between two utterances[2] the operative *something in common* whereby the one influences the other may be any

[1] Adapted with considerable changes from Claude E. Shannon and Warren Weaver, *The Mathematical Theory of Communication* (Urbana: University of Illinois Press, 1949), p. 5.

[2] I need a highly general term here, not limited to any mode of utterance, such as *overt* speech or writing. An act of comprehending may itself be regarded as an utterance, being a rebirth, after passage through the lifeless signal, of something more or less the same as the original which was transmitted.

feature or character or respect whatever and can be itself highly complex. It may be some conjunction of respects. The comprehending of any utterance is guided by any number of partially similar situations in which partially similar utterances have occurred. More exactly, the comprehending is a function of the comparison fields from which it derives. Let the units of which these comparison fields consist be *utterances-within-situations*—the utterance and its situation being partners in the network of transactions with other utterances in other situations which

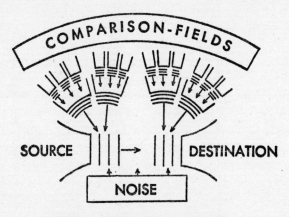

UTTERANCES-in-SITUATIONS

lends significance to the utterance. Partially similar utterances made within very different situations are likely to require different comprehendings, though language is, of course, our collective attempt to minimize these divergences of meaning.

A comprehending, accordingly, is an instance of a nexus [1] established through past occurrences of partially similar utterances in partially similar situations—utterances and

[1] See C. K. Ogden and I. A. Richards, *The Meaning of Meaning* (London: Routledge & Kegan Paul, 1941), pp. 52–59 and Appendix B. The word 'context' there used seems to have been misleading. See my *Interpretation in Teaching* (London: Routledge & Kegan Paul, 1938), p. viii.

situations partially co-varying. The past utterances-within-situations need not have been consciously remarked or wittingly analysed; still less need they be explicitly remembered when the comprehending occurs. Thus the word *comparison* in the technical term 'comparison-field' may mislead. It is not necessary that the members of a comparison-field—widely diverse utterances-within-situations as they may be—should ever have been taken together in explicit analytic scrutiny and examined as to their likenesses and differences. The discriminations and connections (dividings and combinings) which arise in the development of meaning are, in some respects, *as though* this had been done. Sometimes they are so produced; but, for the most part, they need no such elaborate reflective procedure. Let me generalize 'comparison' here to make it cover whatever putting together and setting apart (however unremarked) has been operative in the formation of the nexus. The routine of concept formation and of discriminative behaviour even down to what we might call merely perceptual levels has an interesting resemblance to the highest activities of systematic conceptual classification. It is as though the nervous system had been taught Mill's Joint Method of Agreement and Difference.

What I have been sketching applies, for the translator, in the first place to the Decoding and Developing of the Chinese utterance. In the second place it applies to the Selecting and Encoding which (it is hoped) will produce an utterance in English acceptable as a translation from the Chinese. But, plainly enough, the co-varyings of utterances-within-situations for English are other than they are for Chinese. Any translator has acquired his Chinese and his English through 'comparison-fields' which are different and systematically different in structure: different not only with respect to the ways in which utterances change with situations, but also with respect to those changes that are significant in utterances (e.g. phonemics) and with respect to those changes that are significant in situations (e.g. status recognition). The comparative linguist could, if he wished, illustrate this for the rest of his natural days. And it is one of the pedagogue's reasons for preferring a 'direct' method to a 'translation' method in beginning language learning. He finds that by keeping to one language only he can provide comparison-fields (through sequences of sentences-in-situations) which are more effective, that is, more propitious to full and deep comprehending later on. This structuring of experience will of course differ with our aim. The linguist—for his purposes —will set up one schema of respects in which comparisons will be made; the pedagogue—for his purposes—will set up another. What schema will a translator set up to serve as a theory of the sorts and interrelations of meanings to guide him in his own tasks?

Limitless in their variety, these tasks present themselves, the words, phrases, sentence forms and the situations, and the meanings, to be compared being as varied as the ways in which they may be compared. How are we to choose the respects (or dimensions) which will serve us best as headings under which to arrange those similarities and those differences of meanings which the translator must try to discern in one language and to achieve in another? In the concrete, in the minute particulars of practice, these comparison-fields are familiar enough; though we tend to forget, as scholars, what we must often, as pedagogues, recall: that these comparison-fields go back into infancy. All we have to do is to arrange, in a schema as parsimonious as adequacy will allow, a body of experience so common that if the purposing of our arrangement could be agreed on, there might be little we would then differ about.

Let us turn our communications diagram through 90 degrees now and look down it. Here is a cross-section of the activities to be found there, made at the points where what is prepared for transmission and what has been decoded and developed may be supposed—in a successful communication—to resemble one another most nearly. I have marked and numbered for labelling the seven[1] divisions in my proposed schema.

Let us label these *sorts of work* which an utterance may be doing with two or more sets of names, academic and colloquial—on the assumption that communication will be made more probable if we use here a multiplicity of largely equivalent indications. I am numbering them for

1. Points to, selects. . . .
2. Says something about, sorts. . . .
3. Comes alive to, wakes up to, presents. . . .
4. Cares about. . . .
5. Would change or keep as it is. . . .
6. Manages, directs, runs, administers itself. . . .
7. Seeks, pursues, tries, endeavours to be or to do. . . .

1. Indicating
2. Characterizing
3. Realizing
4. Valuing
5. Influencing
6. Controlling
7. Purposing

convenience of reference; but I do not want to suggest that there is any fixed temporal order, that first we Select, then we Characterize, then Realize, then Value, then would

[1] A possible eighth division might be Venting (that one of the multifarious meanings of the word *expression* which seems least well covered by my seven). Utterances from a simple 'Ouch!' or 'Ooh!' up to *The Divine Comedy* can be regarded as drive-reducing—in terms, that is, of the psychology of the utterer. But, since the purposes of a psychological investigator are not those of a translator, I would expect different schemas to be suitable. And to me, at present, this respect seems well enough taken care of—for the translator's purposes—through my seven which may *all* in their varying ways be drive-reducing. I am indebted to Dr. Irving Singer for making me see the need for this note, and to Charles Morris' *Signs, Language, and Behavior* (New York: Prentice-Hall, Inc., 1946) for suggestions contributing to my schema.

Influence, then Organize and then Purpose. Nor is there any constant logical order. Let us keep these jobs as independent one of another as we can. In individual cases we will find many sorts of detailed dependence, but let us put none in by definition.

In applying this schema to translating, we can ask of two utterances in two languages:

1. How far do they pick out the same (or at least analogous) things to talk about?

2. How far do they say the same (or at least analogous) things about them?

3. How far do they present with equal vividness and/or actuality, weak or strong?

4. How far do they value in the same ways?

5. How far would they keep or change in the same ways?

6. How far are the dependencies and interplay between 1, 2, 3, 4, 5, and 6 itself, the same in them both?

7. How widely would they serve the same purposes, playing the same parts, within the varying activities they might occur in?

Let me label this sevenfold event which my diagram depicts COMPREHENDING, as comprehensive a name as I can find. Any full utterance does all these things at once, and invites all of them in the comprehender. In some instances, however, one or more of these dimensions, aspects, powers, functions, jobs, variables, parameters, components, ingredients, tasks, duties (all these words are in need of the comparative study my diagram should be an instrument for) will shrink toward the null, the vanishing point. There is swearing and there is mathematics. In swearing there *may* be nothing but 4, 5, and 7; in mathematics only 1, 6, and 7 may matter. It would appear that 7 never lapses; without purposing, without the feedforward[1] which structures all activity, no utterance and

---

[1] See X, pp. 119–122 below; and *How To Read a Page*, Index: 'Purpose'.

no comprehending. A full comparison between two utterances (between an original and a translation of it, for
example) would require us to discern what all their
dimensions, aspects, functions may be and compare them
as to each and as to their relations within the entire comprehending. In comparing boxes or rooms, we need three
dimensions; in comparing comprehendings, we need, I
suggest, at least these seven.

Even of a single comprehending we can ask our seven
sorts of questions: Under 1, we ask WHICH things are
being talked (thought) of? Under 2, WHAT is being said
of them? Under 3, EVEN SO? Under 4, SHOULD this be
so? Under 5, WON'T YOU (WON'T I)? Under 6, HOW?
Under 7, WHEREIN, WHEREBY, and WHEREFORE, TO WHAT
END?

Of these, 1 and 2 may be felt to be more narrowly, more
clearly, *questions* than the others; and 3 especially may seem
to be rather a wondering than a questioning. Under 3,
what is in question is the nearness and fulness with which
something is to be present to us. *Doubting* ('is this so or
not, possibly, probably, certainly?') belongs (in this
schema) rather to 5 or 6 ('to be accepted or not, and
how?').

Let us consider these functions in turn.

Indicating and *Characterizing* will need less comment
than the others. They have been more discussed, for they
correspond to the distinction logicians make under the
labels 'Extension-Intension' and 'Denotation-Connota-
tion'. In the logicians' use, the denotation of a term is
whatever may be covered by the term and the connotation
is the set of properties (characters) anything must have if
it is to be so covered. But there is also a well-established
literary use of 'connotation' in which the connotation is
3, 4, and 5 in my diagram rather than 2 (which is likely
then to be called the 'bare, or mere meaning'). These two
uses of 'connotation' parallel what may be the chief differ-

ence between scientific and poetic use of language. There is some parallel, too, with what I have discussed (*Interpretation in Teaching*, p. 311) as the rigid and the fluid uses of language. If we make Characterizing be '*saying something about* what is being pointed to', we have obviously to narrow down the meaning of 'saying'. It can open out to take in anything that an utterance can do, anything in any way said, suggested, evoked, hinted, required, and implied (the literary connotation), or it can be kept down to the logician's connotation—the 'definition' (as it is sometimes put) of a term.

The last paragraph illustrates—as must any attempt to write about the language we use or should use about language—the heavy duties we have to put on quotation marks. I have suggested (*How To Read a Page*, pp. 68–70) that we should develop sets of specialized quotes, as a technical notation by which we could better keep track of the uses we are making of our words, and I have tried out the use of a few such quotation marks in that book and elsewhere. I am now more than ever persuaded of the usefulness of this device. It can serve us to distinguish many different uses we make of quotes. For example:

^{w} . . . ^{w} to show that it is a word—that word in general, Peirce's ^{r}type^r—which is being talked of.[1] For example, ^{w}use^w is a highly ambiguous word.

^{oc} . . . ^{oc} to show that occurrences of a word—Peirce's ^{r}token^r—are being talked of. For example, I have been using ^{oc}uses^{oc} above in various ways.

^{r} . . . ^{r} to show that some special use of the word or phrase is being *referred* to. The marks may be read as *refer to* and the implication may be that only by having that particular use of the word in that passage present to us in lively attention (Realizing) can we distinguish it from other uses and avoid confusion.

[1] *Collected Papers of Charles Saunders Peirce* (Cambridge: Harvard University Press, 1933), IV, 423.

^{t} . . . ^{t} to show that the word or phrase is being used as a *technical term* anchored by a definition to some state of affairs or procedure—to an operational technique perhaps or to a set of performances.

$^?$ . . . $^?$ to show that how the word or phrase is to be comprehended is the question. It may be read as *query*; and we can develop this notation further by adding 1–7 after the ? to show where the focus of the question lies in my diagram. These ?'s should carry no derogatory suggestion; their work is to locate and orientate inquiry; they are servants of **6**. Thus we might write $^{?2}$connotation$^{?2}$ or $^{?3, 4, 5}$connotation$^{?3, 4, 5}$ to direct attention either to the logical or to the literary questions.

^{sw} . . . ^{sw} to show that we are considering what may be *said with* a certain word or phrase without decision as yet to what that is. This enables one to bring together meanings of words and phrases, for examination, without settling anything prematurely as to how they may be related. We need to bring these meanings together *before* we pick out those we may profitably compare. I have written elsewhere at length (*Interpretation in Teaching*, ch. xv and xix; *How To Read a Page*, ch. x) on the troubles which the lack of such a warning mark may lead us into.

$^!$ . . . $^!$ to show astonishment that people can write or talk so. Some will want to put this whole paper within such marks.

Once we recognize to what an extent thinking is a taking care of and a keeping account of the conduct of our words, the need for a notation with which to study and control their resourcefulness becomes obvious.

^{sw}Indicating^{sw} or ^{sw}Selecting^{sw}—especially if we picture it to ourselves with the image of a pointer (an arrow as of a wind vane)—may seem instable. It can be so; but some of our selectings are the most constant things we do. Angus Sinclair puts a further point well: 'What is thus loosely describable as the selecting and grouping which each of us carries out is not an act done once and thereby completed, but is a continuing process which must be sustained if our experience is to continue as it is. If for any reason it is not sustained, i.e. if for any reason a man follows a different way of grouping in his attention, then the experience he has will be different also. Further, this requires some effort. . . . Knowing is not a passive contemplation, but a continuously effort-consuming activity.'[1]

Sinclair's ˢʷgroupingˢʷ seems to be my ˢʷCharacterizing, Sortingˢʷ. We have, in English, what may seem an excess of analytic machineries to help us in distinguishing |its| from |whats|, that is, Indicating, I, from Characterizing, 2. Such are (in most uses): for I, ʷsubject, substance, entity, particular, thing, being, group, classʷ; for 2, ʷpredicate, attribute, property, quality, relation, character, essence, universalʷ. A large methodological question which can seem to fall near the very heart of any endeavour to translate philosophy is this: does use of different ʾanalytic machineriesʾ entail difference of ʾviewʾ? I put my ?'s in here to remind us that both ˢʷanalytic machineriesˢʷ and ˢʷviewˢʷ have to do with little-explored territories though they are surrounded by the most debatable land in ʾthe Western philosophic traditionʾ. Current use of most of this machinery is erratic: at a popular level it cares little which of the above words are employed; more sophisticated use varies from one philosophic school to the next.[2] There is little likelihood of increased clarity unless some new factor enters. The exercise of choice required when thinking which is remote from ᑫthe Western philosophic traditionᑫ—thinking which uses, perhaps, no such machinery—has to be thoroughly explored in English, might be just such a new factor. The distinction between Indicating and Characterizing, and their queer inter-play, might, through translation studies, become again the central growing point for thought.

[1] Angus Sinclair, *The Conditions of Knowing* (London: Routledge & Kegan Paul, 1951), p. 35.

[2] See my *Interpretation in Teaching*, chap. xxi, 'Logical Machinery and Empty Words'.

Realizing, 3, needs more discussion here, though what the discussion should bring out is something familiar to everyone. The two meanings we separate most easily in this cluster are exemplified by: (*a*) 'She realized how he would take it' and (*b*) 'He thus realized his ambition.' It is with (*a*) that we are concerned, though the background influence of (*b*), ˢʷrealizingˢʷ as ˢʷthe becoming actual of the possibleˢʷ, is frequently apparent. This duality may be as relevant to Chinese modes of ²knowledge² as it is to some Aristotelian doctrines of becoming.

Within (*a*), two lines of interpretation offer themselves: (i) it may be taken as equivalent to ˢʷShe imagined vividly and livingly how he would feelˢʷ; or (ii) ˢʷShe foresaw how he would actˢʷ. (The vagueness of ᵒᶜtake itᵒᶜ reinforces the ambiguity of ᵒᶜrealizedᵒᶜ.) This exemplifies a frequent shift in ˢʷrealizeˢʷ: the shift between a lively, concrete, actualized presence and a cognizance of implications and consequences which may be (and commonly is) highly schematic. A statesman may realize what the outcome will be all the better for not realizing too vividly how X may feel. It thus appears that while the use of ʷrealizeʷ in (i) does entail a high degree of Realizing, 3, in my schema, ʷrealizeʷ in (ii) does not. The entirety of apprehension which is ascribed by remarks such as 'He fully realized', and the contrast with 'He didn't at all realize', can be handled in terms of 1, 2, 5, and 6.

What is highly realized may be distinct, explicitly structured, detailed, ²definite² in most of the senses of this strategic word.[1] But it may equally well be very indefinite. That unlocatable, indescribable, almost unidentifiable qualm which is the first emergence of nausea is something which can be Realized to the full without as yet being Characterized in any but the sketchiest fashion. Conversely, Characterizing may be most complete and minute without much Realizing having developed. In

[1] See *Interpretation in Teaching*, ch. ix, ' "Definite" '.

fact, fullness and detail in Characterizing frequently prevent our Realizing, though the details may be offered expressly to increase it. On the other hand, many devices —from headlines to the routines of the dispatch editor and the commentator—reduce the reality of what is presented. Much that is called 'sensationalism' has this effect. We may suspect that this is sometimes its justification. We need to be protected from the wear and tear of actuality. It would not be surprising if this wrapping-up professed to be unwrapping.

> Human kind
> Cannot bear very much reality.

None the less, increase in Realizing is in general accompanied by increased particularity in Characterizing, and by increased choosiness and discrimination in the Selecting of what shall be Characterized.

Realizing is very frequently brought about through metaphor, as may be illustrated by the following vivid account of a moment of Realization from Virginia Woolf: 'Suddenly, as if the movement of his hand had released it, the *load* of her accumulated impressions of him *tilted up*, and *down poured in a ponderous avalanche* all she felt about him. That was one sensation. Then *up rose in a fume* the essence of his being. That was another. She felt herself *transfixed* by the intensity of her perception; it was his severity: it was his goodness.'[1] (My italics.)

Metaphor, however, can serve under all my headings. It is worth remarking with regard to Chinese–English translation that the great traditional metaphors of Western thought play so large a part in shaping our conceptions that a study of any metaphors which have played a comparable part in Chinese thought suggests itself as possibly a key move. Examples in the Western tradition would be: the metaphor of conception used in the previous sentence

---

[1] *To the Lighthouse*, p. 41.

(see *Phaedrus*, 276E); the analogy of the Self and the State from the *Republic*, and the tripartite structure of both; that other Platonic metaphor of intellectual vision, the eye of the mind; the comparison of the idea of the good with the sun; the metaphor of light as truth generally; the metaphor of inspiration; and, from Hosea, the metaphor of a marriage contract between the Lord and Israel, and indeed the use of the ideas of love (not sex) and fidelity in theology. These great originative structurings have acted in the West in innumerable minds which have had no notion of how important such metaphors can be. It would be hard to say, indeed, of the Self–State analogy whether thought about personality or about government has been the more influenced by it, for the traffic has been two-way. Where such a metaphor is absent in Chinese or where Chinese has a traditional metaphor which English lacks, the loss in translation is likely to be grave. The remedy is, perhaps, through a deeper, more systematic study of metaphor.[1] Assistance in such studies is, of course, one of the aims of the schema of comparisons offered in my diagram.

Valuing, 4, is a modern philosophic battleground, the dispute being in part whether the language of valuation, obligation, and justification is to be comprehended in some peculiar fashion or fashions (as !'emotive?!) or in the ordinary way of description. For the purposes of comparative study of meanings, this warfare, on which so much time and talent is being spent, may not be important. It is not clear that any decision would help us to compare meanings better. It may be wise to hold that: 'Evaluations are a form of 'empirical knowledge',[2] which might put considerable strain on our concepts of 'empirical knowledge'; or it may be wiser still to hold that will and desire may enter into valuations in more ways than those in

---

[1] See my *Philosophy of Rhetoric*, Lectures 5 and 6.

[2] C. I. Lewis, *An Analysis of Knowledge and Valuation* (La Salle, Ill.: Open Court Publishing Co., 1946), p. 365.

which they enter our type specimens of empirical knowledge. To decide which view would be wiser, we would
have to be able to make comparisons between meanings
beyond our present scope. What does seem certain is that,
as an instrument for the comparison of meanings, our diagram
should avoid prejudging this issue. It should be able to
represent the opposed positions more justly; they look as
if they were almost equally in need of restatement. But
notice here how ᵒᶜshouldᶜᵒ and ᵒᶜjustlyᵒᶜ and ᵒᶜin need ofᵒᶜ
appear in this very remark. Any formulation of these
considerations is itself valuative as well as factual; the
conflict it hopes to adjudicate is alive in the bosom of the
judge. The difficulties ensuing from this I shall discuss
under Aspect 6, the Management, Control, or Administration of Comprehending. Meanwhile, my diagram
assumes that ˢʷValuingˢʷ is different from Realizing,
Characterizing, and Indicating; and that it 'should' be
defined in such a way as to avoid implying any fixed
relations to them—though, of course, the interplay between all three will be varied, incessant, and all-important.
All study of language and thought *in action* is both an
exemplification and enjoyment of this kind of interplay.

As another precaution, we may leave the full variety of
Valuing unconfined. We are concerned here not only with
all the attitudes which may be uttered by the aid of ʷgoodʷ
and ʷbadʷ, ʷrightʷ and ʷwrongʷ, ʷbeautifulʷ and ʷuglyʷ,
ʷpleasantʷ and ʷunpleasantʷ, ʷimportantʷ and ʷtrivialʷ,
but with the ranges of love and hate, desire and fear,
hope and despair, belief and disbelief. These fields are
all polar, and there is a middle zone where it may be
doubtful whether any valuing is going on and whether it
is positive or negative. So Valuing may often seem to
lapse.

Similarly, and perhaps as a consequence, Influencing,
5—that part of a Comprehending which endeavours
either to change or to preserve unchanged, to be changed

or to remain unchanged—may be too slight to be re-marked. If we ask what it is here which would change or be preserved, it may be best to reply ˢʷthe onflowing situationˢʷ and to remind ourselves that this ˢʷonflowing situationˢʷ is at least twofold. It is (*a*) that motion of affairs within which the Comprehending is proceeding; it is also (*b*) the Selecting, Characterizing, Realizing, and Valuing, and the rest, through which the Comprehending is taking account of and dealing with (*a*). It is what is happening *and* what we take to be happening. We are lucky when these sufficiently accord. Influencing—the keeping of the stream of events so or the changing of it—concerns (*a*) as offered to us in (*b*) and, within (*a*), it includes our adjust-ment to the not-us as well as the adjustment of the not-us to ourselves. In general, a Comprehending is concerned to change part of the onflowing situation and keep the rest unchanged. Something has to remain unchanged; there has to be some continuant, if change is to be possible: so at least we may be wise to suppose.

Controlling or Administering, **6**, has to do with these decisions as to what it will be wise to suppose, and with what arises through these supposals. Wisdom, we may remember, 'lies in the masterful administration of the un-foreseen.'[1] We may be highly surprised to discover what we are supposing. The supposals may be conscious, and arrived at through explicit reflection and deliberation and choices wittingly made, or they may be unwitting, picked up from the tradition or from the accidents of habit forma-tion. And they may concern every aspect of meaning—from Selecting round to Controlling, this would-be executive, itself. Many of our most important supposals concern the nature of meaning and the connections of the sorts of meaning with one another, in brief, the very topic our diagram should help us to explore.

---

[1] Robert Bridges, *The Testament of Beauty* (Oxford, 1939).

It is here, in this aspect of the mind as a self-ordering endeavour, as a government hoping to maintain itself,[1] that compromise appears most clearly as the practical art of the translator. To ask: Where in general will compromise be most needed? is to try to divide the fields of possible discourse. There are areas of settled routine—much of trade, for example—where the fixed and comparatively simple structuring of the things and events to be dealt with allows of a fine practical equivalence between the languages used. Wherever there is a clear operational check upon Comprehendings this happy condition is likely to prevail. Mathematics, physics, the strict sciences can be translated without loss—by the introduction of the technical term and the use of the type-specimen, the model and the operational definition. Here functions 1, 2, and 6 are serving a Purposing so general that it can hide behind the ordering, 6, of what is said, 2, about what, 1. But as discourse grows less abstract and hypothetical, more entire and actual, the probability of loss and therefore the need for choice and compromise become greater. With narrative and philosophy and poetry in so far as the growth and history of the language and of other social and cultural institutions enter in, a self-denying statute is required. If we take Ethics to be 'the bringing to bear of self-control for the purpose of realizing our desires',[2] we have to decide which of our desires must give way to which. The translator has first to reconcile himself to conceiving his art in terms of minimal loss and then to balance and adjudicate, as best he can, the claims of the rival functions. His question is: Which sorts of loss will we take in order not to lose what? And answering that is in practice a series of decisions, 6, on behalf of a policy, 7, which may very well have to declare itself openly, in a preface or in footnotes. The mind-state analogy is at work

---

[1] *Republic*, 591.
[2] *Collected Papers of Charles Saunders Peirce*, I, 334.

all through, it will be perceived. The translator is called upon to become a statesman and serve a limitless oncoming state. His chief advantage over his analogue is that he can, sometimes, go back and undo his mistakes. He can cancel and choose again. But for the rest his practical sagacity must accept the hard commonplace truths: if we try for too much, we will get less than we might, and what we can go on to do will depend on what we have done and are doing now.

Translation theory—over and above the aid it may afford the translator—has thus a peculiar duty toward man's self-completion, to use a concept which seems to be suggestively common to the Chinese and the Western traditions. We are not weather vanes, 1; we are not filing systems, 2; we are not even agonies or delights only, 3; we are not litmus paper, 4, or servo-mechanisms, 5. We are guardians, 6, and subject therefore to the paradox of government: that we must derive our powers, in one way or another, from the very forces which we have to do our best to control. Translation theory has not only to work for better mutual comprehension between users of diverse tongues; more central still in its purposing is a more complete viewing of itself and of the Comprehending which it should serve.

III

Emotive Meaning Again[1]

'Dark as midnight in her black dress, her haggard beauty and her unutterable woe, she had looked at me long enough to appear to say that her right to sit at my table was as good as mine to sit at hers.'
                                                   —*The Turn of the Screw*

'After observing the unstudied grace of her movements, the most celebrated painter of the province forsook the implements of his trade and began life anew as a trainer of performing elephants.'
                                                   —*The Wallet of Kai Lung*

'No amount of calculation will create an obligation or anything like it. . . . When Music weeps, all humanity, all nature weeps with it. . . . Thus do pioneers in morality proceed.'
                                 —*Les Deux Sources de la morale et de la religion*

IN a completely neglected book[2] written over a hundred years ago, Alexander Bryan Johnson has a sentence which will win the sympathy of all who have written on these matters. 'As, however, the following sheets are the painful elaboration of many years, when my language or positions shall, in a casual perusal, seem absurd (and such cases may be frequent,) I request the reader to seek some

---

[1] This essay formed part of 'A Symposium on Emotive Meaning', *The Philosophical Review*, March 1948, the other participants being Max Black and Charles L. Stevenson. I wrote it with Max Black's contribution before me and am indebted to him for allowing me to add excerpts from his article to make the points I reply to fully intelligible.

[2] *A Treatise on Language* (republished in 1947 by the University of California Press), p. 28.

more creditable interpretation.' In quoting this I have in view my own efforts to interpret quite as much as Max Black's. May I read him as well as he reads me! There are, however, one or two points, where doubtless my language was unclear, and some over-all strategic considerations which my early pages tried but failed to present. A few comments on these may be a good way to prepare for what I would not call a renewed attack on, but rather a resumed courtship of, this coy and probably cozening problem.

I am heartily in accord with Black that the bandying about of 'emotive' has done more harm than good. The word was a label which early encapsulated its topic, protecting it from inquiry. In my experience, when this happens, the fault is not with the label but with the topic or with the type of inquiry against which the topic is protecting itself. Here I blame both the topic and the inquisition it could expect if its defences were dropped. The topic did not want to grow up, and the police wanted a conviction.

This is, of course, to use the notions and the language of juvenile delinquency studies upon peccant language behaviour. Such metaphors may seem odd and out of place. They may even seem subversive—aiming to promote 'an intrusive and pervasive dissolution of structure' in Black's admirably discerning and penetrating phrase. ['R's later doctrines seem to have overcome the doctrinaire rigidity of his earlier nominalistic behaviourism only at the cost of an intrusive and pervasive dissolution of structure. And we seem to be still in as much need as ever of a clarification of the relations between the cognitive and the affective functions of symbolism.' (*Op. cit.*, pp. 121—2.) My query today would be: 'What sort of a clarification? Perhaps that which a play rather than an essay might offer?'] It will seem the more subversive if it can be believed that their user is deliberately attempting with them to replace one type of structure or procedure for these inquiries by another. There may be some difficulty in supposing that anyone can be seriously using metaphor, not as decoration and beguilement, not as a literary grace, but as a technique of reflection and an operation of research. This attempt, however, seems worth making. The study of metaphor, through metaphor, should become, I have suggested, a central and governing part of the study of language. Perhaps one of the reasons why Black finds my later views 'very puzzling' is that I have been trying to practise what as a student of metaphor I have preached.

Here is one of the questions of over-all strategy. Can any present-day, logico-analytic inquiry give us a useful picture (an employable 'speculative instrument') for improving our handling of language? (It is *all* our handling of language—not only our 'discourse about discourse'— which we need to improve.) Black agrees that logico-analytic inquiries—or current *prose* modes of inquiry by whatever name we choose—have not done this. The work remains, as he says, to be done. My question is about what this work is, and whether a 'consistent and coherent theory of emotive meaning', when we arrive at one, could do it. I am asking whether any *prose* theory designed on traditional and current lines can be or provide a suitable instrument. And by stressing *prose* so I have implied (by means which would elude a strictly logical analysis) that *poetic* theory might supply what is lacking. It would not be a prose account of poetry so much as a poetic account of prose—or rather of the mixed mode whose troubles make us write about them here.

Clearly enough, this prose-poetry antithesis I have dragged in here is but the referential-emotive problem back again. I drag it in to protest against the nearly universal assumption that the right means to comprehension and control is an account modelled—as far as possible—

41

on the accounts used in mathematics and the simpler sciences. I see no evidence, prosaic or poetic, for thinking that economy, abstractness, simplicity, and rigour—merits though they be in a logico-analytic treatment and sources of power to it in its appropriate field—are merits at all or sources of power to an account of the jobs or functions of language. I see some evidence to the contrary, though I am not sure of what kind, referential or emotive, this evidence would be. For the answer to that turns on how we *should* conceive these kinds—which is precisely what we are considering. The serpents here unyieldingly bite one another's tails. In brief, let us not suppose too lightly that the business of distinguishing and relating science and poetry belongs to science.

So far, I fear, this contribution will have looked unenticingly like a proposal that readers of *The Philosophical Review* should drop the tools of their trade and begin life anew as poets. There is a little more to it, I hope, than that. And I find comfort in Black's insistence on the place of intellectual understanding in what I suppose we must name 'aesthetic appreciation'. (I wish we could find a less slobbery name for it!) Emotive language can work through intellectual exploration, though it need not always do so. And it can, and regularly does, *present* (to use Black's term) and step toward its further ends through *presentation*, as I believe I have always believed and often maintained.[1]

---

[1] Here, through my fault doubtless, Black seems to have mistaken my view. In *Principles*, not only were poems full of references and commonly built on them, but feelings and emotions had reference too and were 'sometimes a more subtle way of referring' (p. 131). My distinction was between two different *uses* of language: 'A statement may be used for the sake of the *reference*, true or false, which it causes. This is the *scientific* use of language. But it may also be used for the sake of the effects in emotion and attitude produced by the reference it occasions. This is the *emotive* use of language' (p. 267). Compare also *The Meaning of Meaning* (pp. 235 and 239). Note further: 'In reading of poetry the thought due simply to the

The popular sense of ^{w}emotive^{w}—for which I fully share Black's abhorrence—seems to me to be due chiefly to a prejudice as widespread as it is deep that clear and full $^{?}$understanding$^{?}$ is the peculiar aim, privilege, and prerogative of science and that such $^{?}$understanding$^{?}$ can only be developed and conveyed through language which does nothing but refer. Whereby very obvious denigratory implications are attached to ^{w}emotive^{w}. $^{?}$Understanding$^{?}$ here should be, but in sad fact is not, one of the most recognizable of question-beggars. It can cover *all* modes by which we take account of situations: the narrow mode, primarily concerned with accurate prediction, which we call scientific; and the fuller modes for which we need emotive language. The occasion is thus kept up for one of those both-and-yet-neither straddles, those one-foot-in-each-boat manœuvres, which so bedevil semiotics. (And yet how encouraging are the skill and balance evinced, if we could use them to better purpose.) The logician exhibits as $^{!}$nonsense$^{!}$ (in his own sense of that; and he has the hardest time saying what his own sense is) all expressions which do not fit into his formulations. The psychologist dismisses as $^{!}$prescientific$^{!}$ all modes of discussing human behaviour not yet statable in his terms (which change every few years). He bows respectfully to what Tolstoy can give us, but doubts if it should properly be called $^{?}$understanding$^{?}$—a word which he succeeds somehow in uttering as if he understood it. On all sides we see students perched on lofty stepladders of the purest available prose, sampling, examining, analysing, restating, and even appraising (through spectacles designed at least to be of scientific diction) the vast, enigmatic and otherwise con-

words, their *sense* it may be called, comes first; but other thoughts are not less important' (*Principles*, p. 128). I find the phrase 'comes first' unacceptable now. See above, p. 26. It seems to me unlikely that the participations of the ^{rt}respects^{rt} have, in poetry, any fixed precedence (^{rt} . . . ^{rt} as explained above, pp. 29–30).

cerned assemblage of the not-prose. Is it a surprising outcome that the more the semiotician demonstrates, in so-called *scientific language*, that ᵂemotiveᵂ should be an honorific term, the more, in fact, he encourages a disparaging use for it?

Some of this is implicit in Black's remark: 'In popular usage, "emotive" is itself a highly emotive term . . . a debunking term' (p. 112). So too, inevitably, is the correlative term 'referential'. I do not foresee that changes in how we distinguish and relate them, while given in the customary *referential* style (abstract, economy-ridden, simplicity-seeking, and rigour-haunted), will make any difference to these emotive charges. Such forces are little, if at all, influenced by our theories. It is, I fancy, the other way about. And I am sure they influence our practice as theorists[1]—which may or may not accord with our theory. Stevenson makes one of his modestly understressed remarks on this: 'Language about language must share some of the complexities of all language.'[2] I would go so far further as to say that language about the functions of language is likely to *represent* in its own behaviour all their disaccords. It is a perpetual meeting of Secretaries of State.

I am, however, by no means as despondent as this image might suggest. I have proposals for amendment of procedure which I hope may help. And since Black and Stevenson and I seem to agree that we need to construct a new instrument of some sort with which to explore this situation further, let us now try to see what this instru-

[1] As to *Principles*, I regard it still with a benevolent eye as being a better sermon than it knew itself to be. And its attempt to put the causes, characters, and consequences of a mental event in the place of what is known, felt, and willed (p. 262) was *as science*, I think still, on the right lines. It seemed to many readers unintelligible then. Today to similar readers it might seem obvious. In general, what influence the book has had would have been different if more of those who have discussed it had read it. But every author says this!

[2] *Ethics and Language*, p. 80.

ment would have to do. With what do we most need help in our handling of language? This is our key question. I would trace not a few of the semiotician's difficulties to his neglect of it. He has set to work so often without asking what most needs to be done. He has borrowed his tools and his methods without considering whether they will help him to do it. Characteristically he has borrowed from science.

I differ from Black here. His choice of 'the interaction of symbols' as 'the key problem' seems to me to underestimate the human achievement—which is precisely an amazing practical command of these interactions—especially of their syntactic co-operations. I do not believe that word-order, syntactic categories, subordination, or sentence unity are problems which urgently need advancing or that advances here would help much at other points. And as to 'sentence-unity' we should note, I suggest, as with many problems about 'the interaction of words', how the conventions of writing, by separating words, have made them seem to be quasi-independent units possessing —we now imagine—separate 'meanings' which are then modified by their settings. But in practice they get their 'meaning' through the settings they occur in. The separate word's separable meaning is as artificial a construct as the ' "direct knowledge" of a "pure" sense datum' at which Black rightly smiles[1]—however useful for some purposes

[1] Or, I should add, as the 'spatio-temporal particular' which Black, I think in error, finds to have been the standard referent of *The Meaning of Meaning*. Ogden and I did not sniff so hard at universals without sniffing at particulars too (see p. 62, footnote). Compare also: 'Thoughts by this account are general, they are of anything *like* such and such things. . . . We have to think . . . of "something of a kind". By various means, however, we can contrive that there shall only be one thing of the kind, and so the need for particularity in our thoughts is satisfied. The commonest way in which we do this is by thoughts which make the kind spatial and temporal' (*Principles*, p. 128). I draw attention to this page, however, as showing how the view that *thinking is paralleling*, which I have been exploring

the dictionary may show it to be. The problem 'how a series of symbols comes to have the peculiar type of unity associated with *sentences*' is standing on its head. We should be asking instead how a separated symbol comes to be taken as having a meaning of its own.

I grant that the problems of syntax can be very bothersome, or entrancing, to the logician. I would suppose this will ever be so. But, as Black almost points out, these interactions of words provide no problems of interpretation (schoolteachers apart) to a child of five—whose 'deft and sensitive judgment' in *these* matters is encouraging indeed. The problems which do concern us all practically as well as theoretically are, I suggest instead, those of metaphor. Eminent among them are these: What sorts or orders of 'truth' are appropriate to (or possible to) whatever may be 'said' only through metaphor? When and how is what is 'said' through metaphor the same as what is said without it? Is it 'said' in the same sense, or has ʷsaidʷ here taken a metaphoric step? Can we distinguish between *functional* metaphors (those needed in presenting —or promoting—certain meanings) and *ornamental* metaphors[1]? If so, how? Are those senses (or motions) of 'true' which are appropriate to utterances using functional metaphor derived themselves by metaphor from other utterances? Or are they independent?

Thus sparely stated these questions may not seem to extend a very inviting field of study, or one of great practical immediate importance. And yet consider how much of men's most serious and sustained thought and feeling

since, was central to the position from the start. The context theory of reference was a formal sketch of this view. It takes paralleling to be a more fundamental vehicle (*Interpretation in Teaching*, ch. 7) than the push-pulls underlying 'cause'.

[1] For most people who find meaning in sunrises and sunsets, sunrise means birth and sunset death. Much of the poetry of nature is 'conventional' (a blaspheming word here, alas!), and natural signs have a metaphoric lexicography of their own which may be even older than language.

has been focused by religion and what place these problems—of the status of metaphoric thinking and its delimitation—have had, or should have had, there. Or consider how far metaphor has been operative in thought and feeling about the state, in the attitudes which make up nationalism; or what part extensions of ideas developed originally about persons have played in law, for example; or how far loyalties to people get themselves paralleled as fidelities to ideas. Or—to face the other way now amid these streams of traffic—consider the incessant intervention of ideas of space and of physical performances in our thought and talk about the mind—as when we endeavour to 'grasp' or 'apprehend' or come into mental 'contact' with, or 'see' what is being said. Without these 'transferences' of ways of thinking which are at home only in one 'world' of discourse to another world, in which we agree they have no more than a metaphoric 'application', how much of common sense or of our traditional 'picture' of ourselves and our relations to anything would hold together?

I have put my little shrieks,[1] in place of conventional quotation marks, around the words here which most patently 'depend' on metaphoric action. The reader will have no difficulty in finding others on this page which equally rate them. 'Metaphor' itself is, of course, the prime example, a fact which may be of some consequence. But shriek marks may suggest something derogatory, a suspicion, at least, that we would do well to replace these words, if we could, by others which would work without metaphor. Worse still, they may suggest that we should excogitate some theory of metaphor which would do away with the anomaly by providing for every metaphor a reduction to an equivalent expression belonging to an assumed non-metaphoric norm.

These feelings that a metaphoric thought is to be

[1] See p. 30 above and *How To Read a Page*, pp. 66, 70.

suspected, that it is inherently less trustworthy than a non-metaphoric thought, are outcomes of *scientism*—as Black defines it ['belief in the universality of scientific method', p. 120]. My chief point here, with which I hope he may agree, is that until we ?know? vastly more about metaphor it is these feelings themselves which should be suspected. Of course there are plenty of queer fish among metaphors, just as there are among plain statements. But that is not the source for the general uneasiness. The source I think is in ᴺᴮscientismᴺᴮ.[1] And I only put shrieks instead of little NB's around those words in order to draw attention to this point.

Language works emotively, of course, in other ways than through metaphor; and, conversely, metaphor very frequently is not more than referential in use. None the less, as soon as we look closely into the concrete detailed working of language we will be struck by the degree in which men pursue their further-than-referential aims through metaphoric means. And, in practice, field investigations into how people interpret metaphor become hard to distinguish from inquiry into their responses to emotive language. The speculative instrument we are in quest of must suit both purposes, which brings us back to our key questions: *For what do we need this instrument?* and *What sort of an instrument therefore should it be?*

Into any *short* answer to the first of these questions the very problem itself is extremely likely to enter unresolved. For example, it does so if we answer: In order to *understand* the distinction.[2] For ᵂunderstandᵂ, as we all well

[1] I would like to defend my early writings from the charge of scientism, but there are more important things to do. That they have been read as supporting scientism I admit. But in sum their burden is sufficiently against 'the vain attempt to orient the mind by belief of the scientific kind alone' (*Principles*, p. 280).

[2] 'The problem is how to understand the distinction without constructing a misleading scaffolding of unsupported and mythical theory' (Black, p. 120, footnote 19). This could be the ?understand? of know-*how*—as when we

know, equally invites us, (*a*) to develop a referential account, 'a consistent and coherent theory'[1] of the two sorts of meaning; or, (*b*) to preach ourselves a sermon, as eloquent as we can make it, on man's duties to God and man so far as these may be word-borne and word-furthered (whether or not they are also word-fathered and word-born); or (*c*) to do something else.

Of these, (*a*), I have tried to suggest, sacrifices emotive meaning by example; and (*b*) seems unlikely, at this juncture, to be either forthcoming or effective—not though it disguised itself in scientific overalls. What might (*c*) be? Some mixture of explanation and exhortation perhaps? But mixture, unless some better means of co-operation is introduced also, will only I fear increase the strife. We are returned to our quest for an instrument.

This instrument must be able to mediate, it must have a foot in each boat and yet be run away with by neither. And yet again, it must leave both functions free, in the sense that it is their creature and has no support or authority which does not derive in the end from them. It can be no more than an agency through which they may keep themselves from illegitimate mutual interference. And yet, lastly, it has to be the legislature and the judge too, and decide as to which of their interactions are lawful. All this looks like an impossible assignment. It looks also remarkably like the traditional assignment of Reason,[2] or,

---

understand a projector, i.e. know how to run it. As to scaffolding, I would still hold, with Bradley, that we cannot do without some. The only way I know to make it less misleading is to change it while leaving the building unchanged.

[1] Black, p. 112.

[2] Perhaps 'practical reason' would now be a better name. Stevenson puts his finger neatly on what I would call *the* problem, when he writes: 'I know no sense of "practical reason", half attitude and half belief, that I find intelligible.' But I fancy here that the word ᵣintelligibleᵣ is speaking as a partisan of ᵣbeliefᵣ. We need a bipartisan approach. The etymology of ᵂbeliefᵂ may have some relevance here.

equally, like the highest function of the central nervous system.

We seem, in fact, to be in much the same ridiculous position in which Socrates found himself in the middle of Book IV of the *Republic* (432). What we have been seeking has been under our feet (or back of our eyes) all the time. To distinguish, relate, and mediate between the modes of language, or the species of meaning, we need no more than, and no less than, Philosophy. It is a dismaying conclusion to an age much more aware of the perils than of the powers of the study and radically in disagreement as to what Philosophy should be or how it should proceed. It is a conclusion, however, very suited to this Review. But perhaps this way of redefining Philosophy, as the study whose business it is to mediate between the modes of language, may encourage others than myself. It is, at least, my way of whistling in the dark. And with the help of another hint from Plato I can even see something not unlike a dawn.

The Guardian was to be a product of an education designed with the needed care to fit him for his office. What studies will best prepare the instrument *we* have in mind? I have argued that neither theory separately, nor suasion will do it—nor yet a mere mixture of the two. What remains then? A method of inquiry and a technique for judging which is familiar in many fields and indeed characteristic of the learned professions. Somewhat oddly, it seems to be without a recognized general name or even a distinguishing prescription. Perhaps, though, there may be a reason for the absence of this prescription. For when I set myself to write one, as a mere putting down of what I see, I am brought back again to Socrates' embarrassment at having to come out with the definition of Justice. This remedy so painfully sought turns out to have been in full sight all along, familiar to oblivion point, obvious to non-existence, and veritable to incredibility.

Keeping things in their proper places is indeed all we have to do.

Before training for this supreme task can be effective certain conditions have obviously to be fulfilled, certain aptitudes must be active in the student. Vigilant field observation; responsive immersion in the actual, in its full concreteness, before, during, and after the passage of the abstractive processes which yield perception; endlessly returning, self-correcting care for the *how* as well as for the *what* and the *why* and the *whither* of the concern, the wondering itself; an unwinking lookout for analogues in all respects however remote, and avid curiosity about all modes of analogy and parallelism; unfailing symbolic lubrication, keeping the formulation and the form, the name and what it names, the cry and the pang, the command and the desire . . . the utterance and what it utters . . . from jamming together; and, above all perhaps, an itch to see how things look from other angles; these—with enough drive behind them—are among the necessary foundation virtues on which the training works. I have phrased them as ideals here, but all training presupposes them as actuals in some measure, however imperfect. Though they can be developed, we may doubt, with Plato, whether they can be induced. Description of them, however, feels otiose, as any description of reflection does, since those who understand know already.

The training which requires these virtues advances them by recognizing them—that is their chief reinforcement—and by affording them opportunity for exercise. Their nature settles what will do them most good. Their first need is an abundant provision of examples of skilled and less skilled interpretations, specimens of minds at work in the interactions of words undergoing, experiencing, enjoying, checking, comparing, and recording them. There are various ways of collecting this material.

To some degree ordinary discussions can provide it—

especially when the discussions are examined rather than taken part in—when they are treated *as examples*, in fact. What they exemplify is what the growing governor has to learn. That learning is its growth. Taking part in discussions, though a little of this is a necessary phase of the training, is rarely profitable. Nor is a partisan attention to discussions. In view of the immense traditional vogue of the disputation—the belief in and practice of the 'puppy war' with words (*Republic*, 539), which has been 'the rule' ever since Plato's time—this is a point I should stress. No verbal institution has done more than disputation to frustrate man, to prevent the referential and emotive functions coming to terms, and to warp the conduct of language—in its highest self-administrating activities most of all. For a very clear reason. The disputant's interpretations are controlled by immediate specific purposes. He is commonly too busy making his points to see what they are. He is in the worst possible condition to observe what is taking place. And seeing what is taking place is no small part of the business of learning how to keep things in their places.

The conventional patterns of discussion and dispute, the combative tone and conduct of so much philosophical literature, and the pretences that its procedures suggest developments, clarify ideas, or settle points, that they expose errors rather than generate them, that they sieve the grain from the chaff, that they deepen insight rather than obscure it . . . all these suppositions do no great credit to human sagacity on what should be its most enlightened levels. *Corruptio optimi pessima*. The perversion takes subtle forms, and this is one of them. Argumentative prowess, versatility in intellectual manœuvre, and trenchancy in abstract debate offer temptations hard to resist. Whence it comes that academic exercises in philosophy have rarely had more to do with inquiry into truth than training for the tournament or the prize ring. An old complaint this is, echoed down the ages by many who themselves were apt to pursue these idle belligerencies with the most ardour. It is odd indeed how the artificialities of these ancient rituals are maintained, how writer after writer will lay on at his opponent with words like *know* and *true* and *say* and *be*, *mean* and *believe* and *understand*—as though such strokes of tongue or pen could hit anything, and as though finding out how these words may in fact work were not, after all and underneath all, the for ever neglected though ostentatiously paraded aim of the entire performance.

Having noted this—in, I trust, sufficiently dispassionate terms—as a main cause for the backward state of the inquiry into the functions of language, I should point out the great value, in the training for this inquiry, of collections of interpretations made expressly for the purpose. Few who have not made and worked upon such collections realize how much light a variety of verbal responses to a common stimulus can shed upon one another. Such collections, systematically arranged, may well come to have a leading part in the work. It would not be surprising if graded and sequenced sets of such exhibits, working models as Stevenson calls them—a zoological museum of them—proved more *instructive*, more the *instrument* we have been seeking, than any number of analyses, treatises, or diatribes. This, at least, was the hope which led me from my early writings[1] to the composition of *Practical Criticism* and *Interpretation in Teaching*. I did not then foresee how far, in trying to construct such sequences of working models—those especially in which the interactions were metaphoric—my own notions about inquiry and exposition, and later my practice, were going to be changed.

[1] And yet, in rereading *Principles* as Black's article has forced me to do, I am more impressed by its anticipations of my later views than by the occurrence of anything to retract. I changed my vocabulary and my metaphors somewhat, as he noticed, to present much the same views again.

The strangest thing about 'discourse about discourse' is that it forgets so often that it is discourse itself and must therefore illustrate much that it is talking of. And yet its virtue, its *arete*, surely is to know what it is doing, 'know what it is about' as the inspired idiom has it. This peculiar self-knowledge by a phrase of its own functions in the exercising of them—so my phrases and those I read, in our moments of intimacy, tell me—is their only sanction or guide; they are lost without it. Only a knowledge of what they are doing will tell them how to do it. Only that will tell them what to do (as means) and, still further, what they *should* do (as their end). Only that, in sum, will let them mind their own business and not infringe the business of other phrases to a mutual corruption. Only that will keep them just. This self-knowledge, they assure me, they find excessively hard to secure and maintain. The phrase 'self-knowledge' is especially apt so to complain and to hint besides that it is in need of help from me. I have, of course, to direct it for that to other phrases using the first person, but these, it seems, are many of them notorious as self-assertive bullies, violent disruptors, in the great confraternity of the language.

This paragraph has again been using, of course, the key parable of the *Republic*, the founding metaphor one might call it of Western philosophy, the parallel of the mind with a community. To take it as seriously as Plato (for a time at least) took it, to step it up from a city state to a world government (thus undoing the torsion of war), to profit from our accumulated experience of government, from our improved psychology, and from I Corinthians xiii, and to apply all this now to the inter-relationships of our studies, and their techniques: this seems the best way of reconceiving the problem of emotive meaning. And if science—as the exclusively referential mode of language—gets itself cast for the role of the U.S.S.R. that too might be instructive. Science is still animated by a revolt against centuries of oppression and frustration from the emotive functions, which have enjoyed privileges and usurped power beyond their due. If reference now aspires to become the world government and to put them in their place or reform them, that is not surprising. But a self-governing community of studies has to ask whether reference is able to say what the place of poetry and religion is, whether it is able to reform them or only able to destroy them.

A civil war between the studies has long been in progress and the statesmanship which can end it is not yet in sight. Most of our griefs, current and traditional, spring from it. The outcomes are in the papers daily and in our private irresolutions and confusions every hour. Science knows how to teach itself, as Communism knows how to make and train converts. The other persuasions are less effective in their larger tasks. I am not sure—my old phrases will not always talk to me—whether regional autarchy ever looked like a solution to me. The sentence Black quotes: 'We need a spell of purer science and purer poetry before the two can again be mixed' (*Prin. Crit.*, p. 3), may be about something else. It may be saying that both science and poetry must know their own jobs better if they are to live without strife together—not that they should have less to do with one another. My inclusion of science among myths—which Black finds so misleading—was a way of saying that science could not be the world government itself but must find a co-operative place thereunder. In a poorly written paragraph which Black rightly finds 'very puzzling' I tried to indicate that place. It would have been better to have pointed to the unique competence of science in accurate prediction and its claim therefore to guide actions which depend upon that. I did hold, *and still do*, that science is true—i.e. that it says verifiable things—but to protect us from thinking that it is 'true' in other and equally important senses is just what we need

Philosophy, our Universal Studies, our world government, for. And ˈmythˈ as I used it[1] should carry no disparagement and imply no contrast. But how to see that it does not is a task for charity between the studies equivalent to taking up the whole duty of man.

[1] 'All views of Nature are taken to be projections of the mind, and the religions as well as science are included among myths' (*Coleridge on Imagination*, p. 177).

IV

The Future of the Humanities in General Education[1]

Even in that certain hour before the fall,
Unless men please they are not heard at all.
                                                                The Fabulists

AMONG the guests at the Conference on the Humanistic Tradition in the Century Ahead, which
formed part of the Bicentennial Celebration at Princeton
last fall, were men and women with good claim to speak
with authority—and still more with responsibility—for
their subject. The occasion was felt to be challenging.
This conference had been preceded by one on nuclear
physics and another on the social sciences; and the skilful
planners of our programme arranged that we should be
aware of this. It was hardly possible throughout the discussion not to wonder where—in the balance of forces
that are shaping the future—the humanities did come in.
Latish in our deliberations, somebody, perhaps unkindly,
said that we had been talking a lot about our traditions.
He questioned whether the physicists or the social scientists had said much about their tradition. He thought they
were more likely to have discussed their *programmes*.
The audience looked, it seemed to me, somewhat uncomfortable at that. But indeed all to whom the humanities

[1] Reprinted from *The Journal of General Education*, Vol. I, No. 3,
April 1947.

matter may well feel uncomfortable—extremely uncomfortable, if not indeed distressed and alarmed—about what is happening and *not* happening in the humanities at present. And they matter—by definition as well as in fact —to every man, woman, or child who aspires to become or remain a human being.

The Conference on the Humanistic Tradition in the Century Ahead is one source of the following remarks. Another which should be mentioned is the course on Homer, the Old Testament and Plato as Sources of Our Common Thought which I am giving at the moment as part of the experiments under way at Harvard towards 'General Education in a Free Society'. The reflections thus prompted sum up to this. The antinomies focused in that title are very far from being resolved, anywhere or by anyone, either in theory or in practice. Certainly reverence and regard for famous books and a backward-looking trust that all will somehow yet be well are, as these very books might teach, an insufficient equipment with which to meet what does seem to be ahead. Conservatism, in a phrase, must continue to be revolutionary in its technique.

In the last hundred years the human race has multiplied threefold. In 1840 there were some 700 millions of us; now we are more than 2,200 millions. In the next fifty years there will be a further and still more critical increase —unless the worst happens meanwhile. Too much reflective attention cannot be given to this fact. It is far more relevant to the problems of our age—and especially to the future of the humanities—than has yet been generally realized. Quantitative factors, unless technique is developed in commensurate degree, can settle qualitative possibilities—disastrously.

Another new fact, even newer and more momentous, is equally relevant, though it is not so easy to state. *Minds have become more exposed than ever before.* (If any point deserves italics, this does.) And this exposure too is undergoing explosive increase. Mental and moral communications, within each culture and between cultures, have suddenly expanded beyond anyone's power to foresee the consequences. The agencies at work—with one exception —hardly need more than mention. They are mass education, with its stress on verbal or nominal literacy, motion pictures, radio, television, modern advertising, and—here is the exception—modern scholarship. These are the new forces which already expose every urbanized mind to a range and variety and promiscuity of contacts unparalleled in history. And this is but beginning. Already some of the effects are showing. It would not perhaps be a culpable exaggeration to suggest that this expansion of our spiritual communications—and the power of minds to influence other minds which goes with it—has already made two wars of a world scale possible. There will at least be no doubt that this new mental exposure makes immense changes necessary in our conceptions of what the humanities have to do and how they can do it. Let us take a brief look at these agencies in action.

Mass education is of course our hope—our one hope, maybe. But in so far as it must use classrooms, how are we to get teachers able to give their pupils any power to select from among the influences to which they become ever more open? Present economic and social conditions repel almost all who might be capable of doing so, and teaching conditions frustrate those whose imagination and devotion still make them enter the profession. And through the decline of the family and for a thousand other well-known reasons there is now incomparably more for the teacher to do. The humanities, being the hardest things to teach, suffer most. They are the hardest to teach because wisdom, which they exist to cultivate, cannot be cut and dried. Much in other subjects can.

Correspondingly the preparation of a teacher in the humanities is the hardest of all—which brings me to the not, as yet, sufficiently vexed topic of modern specialized scholarship. I have to explain its appearance in my list of disruptive agencies threatening the wholeness of present and future minds.

Modern scholarship is a fearful and wonderful as well as an unprecedented thing. It is unprecedented, I believe, in character as well as in scale, though I would listen eagerly to a modern scholar who was interested in just this historical question. Like so much else which should give us pause, modern scholarship is the product of admirably ingenious innovations in technique, on which Thamus' words to Theuth (*Phaedrus*, 275) are to the point: 'Most ingenious Theuth, one man has the ability to beget an art, another to estimate the good or harm it will do to those who are to use it.' The words apply equally to the ingenious doings of the nuclear physicists and to all inventions which may threaten us with nuclear fission of our minds. In scholarly technique the innovations are the modern dictionary, the book index, bibliography, the specialized journal, and the museum. Most of them seem to be eighteenth-century inventions. At any rate, as they affect us today they are recent. And it is relevant to note that Chinese scholarship only admitted an index to a book within the memory of those still living: an index being considered a subversive thing which would lead to superficiality and to disrespect for the teacher's authority—grounded on long and deep familiarity with a corpus rather than on quick glances at references.

However this may be, modern scholarship certainly requires ever more intensive and prolonged training of a sort which is of hardly any value to a teacher in general education. It is training in the administration of a vast body, an illimitable proliferation rather, of facts, comments, opinions, and mere phrases, too extensive and diverse to form, in any mind not of a very rare order, any coherent, much less any directing or confirming, view of essential human purpose. Moreover, since this proliferation proceeds geometrically, training in its administration, as we well know, becomes departmentalized, then sub-departmentalized, and scholarship, in so far as it is *that*, becomes less and less useful to a teacher. It may fit him to continue as a specialized researcher—within 'areas' or on 'points' with no known relevance to any side of the world crisis. It quite certainly does not give him what he needs as a teacher of the humanities—reasonably rich and considered views of a person's human relations to other persons. Worse still, it is intensive distraction from the hard essential task of maturing such views. Worst of all, this training has now become professional qualification offered competitively by rival institutions.

I would not be misunderstood here. This recent achievement of a method by which scholarship becomes accumulative and responsible to a controlled record is one of the glories of our age. It ranks with the partly parallel achievements in mathematics and experimental inquiry. Together with them it holds out infinite promise to man, and must go on. But, for the time being, as with physics, biology, and psychology (on which last I touch later) its present dangers rather than its remote promises should concern us most. It is preventing us from supplying our greatest need—teachers able to help humanity to remain humane.

Literature—a deep enough *and leisurely enough* familiarity with what the best minds have thought and felt about people—used to produce such teachers. Modern scholarship positively gets in the way. The critical apparatus of approach to the great things keeps them from their would-be student. He is daunted incessantly by the thought that somewhere there is something which would, if he only knew it, help him to understand better. He comes to distrust the direct approach, and lives in an unhealthy terror of his ignorance—which will anyhow for all men and to time's end be infinite. He forgets that we do not help ourselves or others by collecting more facts and comments, but by understanding more clearly our problems and theirs. We learn best to do this by reflecting upon such problems and by seeing them through the eyes of the best minds. So we lose our best teachers.

To turn now to mass media. Radio, TV and the screen might provide some remedy for this loss. It is possible to believe, sometimes, that they could become the instruments of our salvation. But we will agree, without difficulty, that they are not that now—for well-known and chiefly technical reasons. Radio, TV and the screen propagate most successfully the most superficial, the most facile, and the least educating elements of a culture. This is partly because, as programmes, they have to *go on*. They have to change, every fifteen minutes or twice weekly. There is no time for what they present to be deeply pondered, thought over, returned to and considered afresh. Therefore, it rarely is worth such reconsideration. But in every culture it has been the things which received the most lasting and recurrent attention—the books re-read again and again, the stories and sayings known and familiar from infancy to old age, the rites repeated throughout a lifetime, the perennial monuments, the enduring ideas, the constant aesthetic institutions—which have done the most part of the work of the humanities. Mass media, at present, replace such continuous shaping forces by an incessantly shifting play of light and confusing impacts. It is not surprising that they are of little help in seeing life steadily and seeing it whole.

For these and other reasons, just when the humanities are more than ever needed and at a decisive turn of human fate, they are becoming through multifarious distraction —ranging from the movie to the graduate school—inoperative and ineffective. But what is this turn of fate? It is the juncture, at last, of the sciences with the humanities. A juncture is a meeting together, a convergence of different principles into one event; it is also a crisis. What are meeting now head on are two unreconciled ways of conceiving man and his good and how to pursue it. Both wish him well, but they differ radically as to how he can be helped. The physical and social sciences alike—being applications of methods of observation and calculation—conceive men as units subject to forces playing upon them *from without*. A man is a complex unit, no doubt—the psychologist is the last man to overlook this—but differences between men are, for science, to be accounted for in terms of past influences (genes, prenatal supply, early nurture, education, etc.) and present conditions. Any inquiry based upon experimentation and comparison develops such a conception; it abstracts, in its own defence, from other aspects. Thus a man's desires and opinions and beliefs, the springs of his action and sources of his triumphs or sufferings, are likewise, for science, to be studied from without. If they are investigable at all by science, they must be public and they must be manipulatable; that is the methodical crux. It is the modes of such manipulation and the resultant behaviour which are really being studied. To the psychologist education is control of *behaviour*. Not unnaturally, therefore, mass influence techniques, by which groups in Germany, Japan, and elsewhere have controlled the behaviour of vast masses of population (though the behaviour was unfortunate), have come to offer—to better hands, no doubt—alluring prospects of doing man good even against his will.

In contrast, the humanities pin a faith, which is experimentally still ungrounded, on the ideal autonomy of the individual man. He is happiest who is least able to be changed from without, as Socrates averred (*Republic*, 381). Man is not a thing to be pushed about, however kindly or beneficently. He is a spirit who learns—not as a slave learns (*Republic*, 536E), but by exercising the freedom which is his being.

I should illustrate this opposition. I may do so best by an extract from page 18 of *Who Shall Be Educated?*, by Lloyd Warner and R. J. Havighurst, though the authors would, I hope, be horrified by the implications I am about to find in their sentences.

We will look at our American social system, which largely controls our behaviour, much as we would at a complex maze in which animals learn to behave. In such a system we must be taught to learn our way around as we grow up if we are to live normal lives and to behave normally as adults. This is true for all the Tom Browns, Katherine Greens, and Joe Sienkowitzes of our society. Growing up consists in learning how to behave, and learning how to behave means acquiring the proper responses to the batteries of social stimuli which compose our social order.

It is the last sentence to which I would draw most attention. Should 'learning how to behave' mean anything like that? To a humanist (or a Platonist) it should mean learning the *what's* and *why's* of human good—what man's duties and responsibilities and his right relations to his fellows are, and learning how to stick to them under the terrible pressures of pleasure and pain—stronger than any lye or potash (*Republic*, 430)—which for ever try to force us from them. We only learn through understanding the differences and connections between things. It is possible, no doubt, to load the phrase 'acquiring the proper responses' with all this moral teaching. If we do so, of course, all is well! And I will only have been expounding for my authors their full intention. But is that what the sentence suggests? Does it not much rather suggest some smooth adjustment to and conformity with current fashions in morals, a facile acquiescence in socially acceptable mass-circulated doctrine?

Speaking of fashions, we need be no very deep students of social science to know that the heaviest massed 'batteries of social stimuli' directed upon young and old today are the ads. I listed advertisements among the disruptive agencies to which minds are now more exposed than ever before. It seems agreed that Goebbels and his gang learnt much from American advertising techniques. Even though we believe in the virtues of immunization to such attacks, we will do well to consider more seriously than is customary what the ads may be doing today to the humanities. Consider Christmas for a moment.

> O never rudely will I blame his faith
> In the might of stars and angels

wrote Coleridge. But how about using the might of stars and angels in an attempt to sell one's wares? What's wrong about that? On a page of both stars and angels, under a caption: '*And the Angels bring* . . .' we look to see what they do bring, and read, '*Heavenly gift robes and lingerie along the moon-lit trail leading to our star-studded Christmas collection . . . LUCKY STAR, above left . . . is all dressed up to go lounging in a cherubic rayon crepe . . . Radelle Constellation . . . shining brightly on the angel's arm, dream gown of celestial rayon . . . matching figure-moulding slip for heavenly array . . .*', not to mention '*panties that lovely women prefer to wear behind the "seens"*,' and lastly, that no insult should be lacking, '*MOONLIGHT MADONNA GOWN!*' To attend for a second seriously to such exploits will make one wonder if he has lost his sense of humour. But it is more unwise never to reflect upon what an incessant exposure to this sort of thing may be doing to us, if only to the language which channels our inheritance. I have shown this ad to a meeting of teachers of English. My chairman, a superintendent of secondary schools in a great city, took a little umbrage. "Didn't it at least show,' he asked, 'that the writer had profited by a sound grounding in the classics?' He seemed to think this was a proper outcome of a literary education.

We fail, I think, to realize how omnipresent these degradations are, or how much they may blur and disable the spiritual organs they play with and for what mean purposes. Was so much so skilfully designed to enfeeble and betray human judgment ever directed on a previous generation? We need men inspired by Irving Babbitt's noble and tireless scorn to go on pointing to them. I will add but two examples:

In my first our hero is sitting—drinking his beer—in his overstuffed chair, his dog at his feet, the radio on, his floor strewn with papers whose headlines read, 'Cities Bombed', 'Famine', 'Air Raids'. The paper still in his hand says, 'Invasion!' Under the picture comes:

IN A WORLD OF STRIFE
THERE'S PEACE IN BEER

In these bewildering times, where can a man turn to replenish the wells of his courage ... to repair the walls of his faith?

Courage—if you please! Faith—I ask you! Is it surprising that such great words as these have become suspect: so that when people hear or see them they assume they are being got at? Where these words are no longer understood, men no longer understand themselves.

My second: Edison Company placarding the subways in wartime with a bright-windowed villa thus legended: '*In a World of Darkness be thankful for the Light Within*' or some such words. The light within—meaning their products! The strange and dismaying thing about all this is that to those responsible it will be the idea that there is anything objectionable here which will be strange. For this is not blasphemy. Would that it were! It is trivialization, which is truly dangerous. Blasphemy provokes. The trivialized mind is supine, at the mercy of slick manipulators. The outcome can be generations of dehumanized social animals in place of self-controlled, self-judging, self-ruling men and women.

Manipulation and exploitation—for the benefit of the operator, or of the subject—that is the chief danger man

66

incurs through the decline of the humanities. The humanities are his defence against emotional bamboozlement and misdirection of the will. The student of science—without the support of that which has been traditionally carried by literature, the arts and philosophy—is unprotected; the main doctrines and positions which keep man humane are insusceptible, at present, to scientific proof. Present-day science, in fact, like dialectic in Plato's day (*Republic*, 539) or popular philosophizing in pre-Nazi Germany, tends to break them down. Without a vigorous and widespread upkeep of the humanities every country comes to be populated chiefly with 'supposititious sons' (*Republic*, 538). And science in the absence of the traditional communal loyalties can only supply their lack by indoctrination in what will probably be (as the samples run so far) nationalistic myths. Dangers due to new weapons will heighten men's susceptibility to such doctrines and also the temptation to teach them. Thus a very gloomy prospect looms up—deriving radically both from the decay of the humanities and from the exuberant vitality of the applied sciences.

It is not, however, the probability of more, and far more destructive, wars which most alarms a humanist. Circumstances are today too easily imaginable in which planetary disintegration would be a welcome release. What is daunting is the possibility that man may be permanently warped through these tensions—that the ideals which made him human may be destroyed—*before* their work can be taken over by science. For that science—or something into which science, given time and education by the humanities, can develop—is the inheritor of their task seems to me a tenet that no true humanist, remembering Book VII of his *Republic*, can yield, any more than he can truly, as a humanist, despair of man.

V

Education and Culture[1]

THE part of Mr. Eliot's *Notes on Culture* which I am venturing to discuss touches on education. With most of his argument I seem to myself to be in reluctant agreement. I agree with his choice of a definition for ˢʷcultureˢʷ. His choice does pick out 'world and imperial problems' and the 'common danger to all the races of the world'. It separates our concern with these from 'the preservation of windmills'. It combines rightly the 'culture of a class' and 'of a whole people'—'two meanings . . . to be kept distinct but always in relation'. It deeply remembers the soil throughout.

Why be reluctant then? Because the outcomes of this view are so black and disheartening. 'The effects of an industrial civilization have combined to deprive the mass of humanity of its native culture.' Mr. Eliot is very deep in these 'commonplaces of observation'; he has no taste for gloom; and I do not doubt that they are as dismaying to him as to anyone. A million disturbances of relative rates of needed change have led us to a condition so grave that the victims are ceasing to know the causes of the trouble. Other, more violent and far wider industrial and technical revolutions are upon us with still more dangerous local accelerations in our ways, still more disastrous to our balance. We are forgetting even what we would be. It

[1] This formed part of a discussion in *The Partizan Review*.

68

looks as though all the cultures everywhere would be replaced by artifacts—advertisement, pulps, comics, soap opera and screen entertainment, televised or direct—the familiar threat to the new leisure—the leisure from which it seemed, not so very long ago, so much might be hoped. And we must fear that the resistances and defences our culture puts up at all levels—mass education, popularization, scholarly toil, research and museum-mindedness—will with the best intentions merely join in the attack, destroying the culture from within as the sales and production pressures converge on it from without.

Facing this darkness, Mr. Eliot has faith to offer us—faith in the possibility of 'a common faith and order'. That prompts to some action no doubt. It has prompted him in all his work, including the writing of these clarifying Notes. I am not underestimating Mr. Eliot's importance as a defender of the faith. I think he has rallied the broken and made the continuance of the struggle possible in countless cases. But reflection, prayer, and patient waiting for a miraculous deliverance is not, he would himself insist, their whole duty for all men. There is much to be done which is being neglected. And with this I come to his remarks on Education.

'Culture', he says, 'is certainly *not* Education, and to think that we can deliberately produce culture by educating a class, or a selected group, or the whole people for culture, is to expect the cart before the horse." One is tempted to remark that this expectation was duly fulfilled when the motor car came! But, more seriously, is not Mr. Eliot, in the definition of ˢʷEducationˢʷ which he is using, doing the very things he so skilfully avoids doing with ˢʷCultureˢʷ—using it in senses which though current and accepted, and therefore indicative and important, are not the senses most needed in this discussion?

Let me grant at once that what he says about Education is true—*for his use of the word*: 'The only affirmation about education, perhaps, that comes within the scope of this paper, is this: that it is only in a very restricted sense that education produces culture—it is more widely true to say that the culture produces the education.' I agree as regards what he is talking about here. Education, *as we have known and practised it*, won't produce even a tolerable *ersatz* culture to replace our dying worlds. I share his view of the 'laborious inefficiency' and the 'spasms of alarm' through and with which 'we endeavour to supply by education and enlightenment' the native culture we are being deprived of. And yet . . . is our failure because of the *in*efficiency, because it is *alarm* and not zeal which moves us, and because we have as yet neither seen clearly what to do in Education nor how to do it? Or is it a brute and insuperable fact in the nature of things that better ways of imparting 'a right notion of what is valuable, of what we mean by success, and of what types of men we admire' are necessarily and for ever beyond human powers of discovery and use?

To be concrete: we are only now beginning to know how to teach well the most teachable things—reading, writing, and mathematics. We are only now beginning to find out, through these humble studies in method, how to avoid the wasteful, stultifying confusions, misunder-standings and aberrations our random undesigned ways of teaching in all subjects promote. I do not say that better ways of communicating the active principles of moral order are yet in sight. I do say that great improve-ments in Education as 'a department of intellectual design' are. And for me this changes the picture, lighten-ing the darkness.

Since what may be called the traditional means of main-taining or renewing the culture are being destroyed by technological change, the remedy, I conceive, is in im-proving our other means. The sense of ᵂEducationᵂ I miss in Mr. Eliot's Notes would make it ˢʷthe study and pursuit of intellectual and moral order[sw]. I am not certain how far this differs from something Mr. Eliot would call by other names. It is not, for me, 'philosophy' in anything less than Plato's sense. It might be *paideia*. It is not something to be brought down but something by which we could be raised. I am glad to be reminded by Mr. Eliot that 'a high degree of culture (or Education) in an equalitarian society can only be attained if the great majority of men can be raised to a level, and kept at a level, which has never been remotely approached in the past'. I agree. But, after reflecting upon it, I conclude that this very difficulty is no deterrent. High things are hard. And I do not see how this greatest of human efforts is to be made wholeheartedly unless the salvation we are seeking is for all.

Mr. Eliot ends on a hopeful note. 'If we can keep our minds clear . . . we shall be working for those changes which really matter.' How to *make* minds clear as well as keep them clear is, I suggest, for us, as it was for Socrates, the key question. Education is an embryonic study still.

VI

The Resourcefulness of Words[1]

DO literary and linguistic studies or discussions of education have any effects commensurate with the needs of the world? Are we fiddling in the burning city? Could our fiddling really make any future city less inflammable?

Let me start by summarizing an address President Hutchins gave at Yale in February 1940. You will see as I go on how wholeheartedly I would like to support the main things he said then, and where my points of difference—if any—come. The main things were that to find the good life, and the good state as a means to that, we must be philosophers, metaphysicians, or students of *dialectic*; and that what metaphysic or dialectic might be is almost forgotten in the educational world. The points of possible divergence are as to what this is and as to how it is to be taught. The last is important—indeed all-important—for if what I would like to call ˢʷDialecticˢʷ were taught differently, a different thing would be taught. Arguments that this or that should be taught mean little unless we are shown *how* they are to be taught.

Dialectic, for me, is a method, not a doctrine. (I do not think Mr. Hutchins sees it as a doctrine.) It is the method

[1] From a Bergen Lecture given at Yale in 1940. My attempt to proceed along the course sketched here became my book: *How To Read a Page*, (1942).

of ordering the intellectual realm. (How the intellectual realm could be united is considered in Pieces III, VIII, IX, and X.) I do not mean that we can teach method without regard for what it is applied to. And where I am most with Mr. Hutchins is where he said: 'The crucial error is that of holding that nothing is more important than anything else, nothing central and nothing peripheral, nothing primary and nothing secondary, nothing basic and nothing superficial. The course of study goes to pieces because there is nothing to hold it together. . . .' And so —'We have nothing to offer as a substitute for a sound curriculum except talk of personality, "character", and great teachers, the slogans of educational futilitarianism.'

Before I go on, may I linger a moment with this delicious word 'futilitarianism'. It is a good illustration of the queer dependencies of one word upon others in the language. Setting aside the -ism, a sinister enough ending in itself, have you noticed how words ending in -arian somehow suggest that the people talked about are some sort of crank or nuisance? Clearly for Mr. Hutchins *Utilitarians* are such. Consider with them Vegetarians, Fruitarians, and Sabbatarians, and add Grammarians. If you don't like Sabbatarians, try Latitudinarians. Dare I mention Rotarians? Or consider Nonagenarians for a moment. We have Octogenarians too and Septuagenarians. Under seventy people don't seem to be so tiresome.[1] Though even younger folk may be Valetudinarians. Even in the beginning Arians as heretics were unpopular enough. Nowadays we have Aryans and Non-Aryans. Which may suggest to you Barbarians. Proletarian too is hardly a pleasing word and possibly Mussolini was not wholly wise when he gave his blessing to Totalitarian.

But to resume. Mr. Hutchins says excellently that we must have something to hold a course of study together.

[1] But a young friend remarked: 'How could I call myself a Sexagenarian! Why, people would think I was a fiend!'

But the question comes, 'What *would* hold a course of study, of the needed scope, together?' Not Metaphysic as I was taught it at Cambridge or as my friends were taught it at Oxford either. Not Metaphysic as it is taught, I believe, anywhere in any university in the world today, or possibly—to be bold where a scholar would tremble—at any place at any time in the world's schools. If you mention Paris in St. Thomas's day, I would suggest that there were then perhaps less disintegrative forces to be restrained and certainly greater social aids in overcoming them. I do not see that Metaphysic as a doctrine, or group of rival doctrines, holds anything together. The subject which at all times has most split men into opposed camps and in modern times has generated most un-bridgeable and irreconcilable misunderstandings seems hardly the thing to appeal to! I don't now propose to define Metaphysics, so treated, as the systematic cultiva-tion of the deepest misunderstandings. But still . . . we must more than hesitate, I would say, before the claim that metaphysic, as it appears in the history of thought, is what we need. Still less will any appeal to a supposedly possible orthodoxy of metaphysical doctrine meet my doubts. It is not any metaphysical doctrine, *as a doctrine*, that will do this trick.

What then? I am going to urge that a certain sort of attention to language might be, in part, what we need. But here I have to be very careful, for misunderstanding is easy.

The kind of attention to language I have in mind can be described as systematic study of *the inherent and neces-sary opportunities for misunderstanding* which language offers. 'Language offers them', I say; but indeed *it insists upon* them. Words could not do their work unless they could rightly mean many more things than any one man in any one view can see them as meaning. The most ordin-ary and usual word must shift it if it is to serve us. And

74

the more usual it is, the more useful, the more important and the more necessary it is for the fabric of our thinking. Only a very special class of words, technical words pinned and locked tight to other words in a mutually defining technical vocabulary, can keep constant to stable meanings. (Even with these, if the metaphysical frame of a vocabulary shifts—as it will—the whole system of interdependent words can be disturbed as to their meanings.) All non-technical words have ambiguity among the conditions of their service to us. They could not begin to cover our needs without it. We are afraid of this. We endeavour with Dictionaries and the Introductory Chapters of treatises to limit and control it. For the most part, very fortunately, in vain. What we should be doing instead—and here is my main point—is to study this ambiguity, not to fear it but to welcome it as our best opportunity for growth in understanding.

As such it is better, more politic and wiser, not to call this versatility of our words by any such evil-sounding name as 'ambiguity'. Let us call it 'resourcefulness' instead.

The most resourceful words in a language are the indispensable words, those which give structure to thoughts and connect them in larger structures. Words like *is*, *being*, *cause*, *whole*, *part*, *same*, *different*, *imply*, *definite*, *some*, *all*, and *important*; *thought* itself, *connection* and *structure* themselves: in brief, the ordinary everyday—nay, the every-other-sentence words of all sharp-edged discussion. Making a list of them would be making a list of the main topics of metaphysics, of the turning points of dialectic. As such they are the unavoidable tools of all explanation and the key terms of all understanding.

And yet, as I have been saying, and as every metaphysical controversy illustrates, they are the words which most occasion misunderstandings. My suggestion that we might find what we need to 'hold a course of study together' (to use Mr. Hutchins's words again) in a certain kind of attention to language is simply that we try a direct and designed inquiry into the resourcefulness of these words.

Such an inquiry, if well *designed* (see Piece VIII) would amount to a study of metaphysic. (I don't know a subject in which study of the resourcefulness of its key terms doesn't amount to the subject, properly studied, itself.) It is perfectly compatible with close attention to selected passages from great books. I would say it required that. But it would be metaphysic approached from a different angle. We would not be attempting to show our students (much less tell them) what Plato or Aristotle really meant. That is a job for a superhuman historian of human thought a million years hence perhaps. We would be trying to help them to see for themselves some of the more important things the great texts may mean. And, since misunderstandings and corruptions of their thought may have played a great part in our tradition, we would be including these also. We would, I suggest, be giving little time to refutation or to the formal logical technique of philosophical proof or contention. Training in that is best given within a technically rigidified vocabulary; and we would above all try to defend our pupils from supposing that one philosophical view must necessarily be irreconcilable with another. This last amounts to throwing aside what has traditionally been held to be the chief business of philosophers. If you think it too drastic I can only confess that my own commerce with the disputatious has left me with a sad conviction that when you are refuting a view you become too busy to see what it is.

What we would aim at is a knowledge of *how* and *why* these central intellectual terms—*being, have, cause, connection, same,* and the like—can shift their meanings and thus give rise to varied misunderstandings. To develop the spatial metaphor here, which being all but unavoid-

76

able should be made as explicit as possible, all these words wander in many directions in this figurative space of meaning. But they wander *systematically*, as do those other wanderers, the Planets. By fixing a limited number of positions, meanings, for them, we may help ourselves to plot their courses. But we should not persuade ourselves that they must be at one or other of these marked points. The laws of their motions are what we need to know: their dependence upon the positions of the other words that should be taken into account with them.

To early astronomers and travellers the wanderings of the planets may have seemed troublesome. Or, more probably, portentous. Full of significance indeed they were! When understood they became the key to all the other motions in the heavens that we have yet ascertained or conjectured. A similar human preference for 'fixities' and 'definites' and 'absolutes' is perhaps the source of some of the opposition which these suggestions may encounter.

I have said that the wandering—the resourcefulness— of these central terms of discourse is systematic. I ought to say a word or two more on that; to be brief, the same misunderstandings endlessly recur. Few people ever commit a new and original misunderstanding. Misinterpretations run to type, to a small number of types. An adequate study of one intellectual mistake can be made to illumine countless other fields where invitations to similar mistakes are offered. It is this which makes insight into *the patterns of resource* able to knit different studies together. The same problems in interpretation arise in them all. We do not at present benefit as we should from the limited variety of our stupidities. This may be, in part, because we have not developed appropriate exercises. Are we perhaps like mathematicians who had never thought of using the working of examples as a technique of instruction?

VII

Toward Practice in Interpretation

THUCYDIDES said that his history would be 'useful to all who wish to study the plain truth of the events which have happened, and which will according to human nature recur in much the same way.' 'This idea', comments Werner Jeager, 'is the absolute opposite of what we usually call the historical attitude mowadays. A true historian, we think, believes that history never repeats itself. Every historical event is entirely individual.'

I take this to be a fair specimen of the challenges which any serious discussion of anything must perpetually offer to a reader. What do we do with them? And if we are teachers what do we ask our students to do with them? Is it unjust to say that we normally use only two ways of meeting them? (1) We stage a fight between the opposing views; or (2)—if we are wiser and recognize that the mixture in the metaphor of '*views* fighting with one another' is itself a warning—we attempt to mediate between them, to show that as views, or positions, they may both be right in certain ways. Are they not seeing things from different angles and thus talking about different things? and so on.

In either case the outcome is usually unsatisfactory. The fight is likely to have the traditional demerits of debate. Both parties become blinder than they need be. The reconciliation is commonly as uninstructive. We may see that the dispute need not have arisen and that there is a way out. We may even find it, hit on the required distinction: e.g. between ¹history¹ as *a stream of individual events*, as such, unique; and ²history² as *a statement of a way in which things occur*, as such, general and recurrent; and so solve the problem—as itself an individual event. But that leaves us, I believe, much where we were. On the very next page, when we run into another problem of nearly or exactly the same type, we will be as likely as before to start a futile fight. At best we may use another *ad hoc* distinction to make another reconciliation, having learned, I suppose, little or nothing of direct service from our struggles with the problem on the page before.

Is there anything else we could do? Could we study these incessantly recurring challenges to interpretation in another fashion—not as individual events, as such unique, but as ways, as such general and recurrent, in which language tempts thought to folly? Language is always under strain. Could we study the characteristic faults the strains cause, learn thus what to expect and so come to the next example of the same type with a technique for dealing with it which *had* really been improved by our previous encounters with the problem?

I am raising here—you will see—precisely the same false opposition with regard to the events in the history of the individual reader's interpretations which arises with regard to events in world history between Thucydides and ʳthe historical attitude nowadaysʳ. (For ʳ. . .ʳ see p. 29 above.) Again there are the two views—that ʿevents will according to human nature recur in much the same wayʾ (while we continue to use language) and that ʿevery event is entirely individualʾ. Again there are the same possibilities: (1) a squabble; (2) a reconciliation through distinction which is *ad hoc* and therefore relatively uninstructive; (3) some deeper understanding of why language poses this type of problem, of why it is so frequent and of how to handle it.

Thucydides' history, he says, 'was written to be a perpetual possession, not as something to be admired only
for a moment.' It was to be a statesman's manual, at hand
whenever the same situations arose. We were, with his aid,
to see through the individual particularities of the events
described, to the permanent necessities of statesmanship,
the laws of the distribution of power. We were not, like
the modern historian, with his vastly developed equipment
for collecting the individual particularities, to be so
dazzled by them as to give each event only individual *ad
hoc* treatment, to be admired or not as such. To press the
parallel with reading: Can an account of a reader's problem and its settling be written so that it may be equally
a ⌜perpetual possession⌝ aiding us to see the permanent
necessities of interpretation, the laws of the elasticity of
language? Can we contrive such a thing as a reader's
manual to help us whenever the same situations arise?
Or must we admit that every problem of interpretation is
unique and must be tackled on its own without conscious
reference to parallel cases?

It is arguable that in Plato's earlier dialogues we have
just such studies in interpretation—analogues of Thucydides' history—examples of verbal situations treated so
as to bring out and provide, as a ⌜perpetual possession⌝,
insight into the permanent laws of the behaviour of words.
We can invent a modern philologist to be the analogue
of the modern historian—so enthralled by his ability to
reconstruct and display the probable social determinants
of Plato's thought that the very possibility of a general
import escapes him. At best, a general import may seem
a vain hope—pardonable, of course, in an early thinker.
We have since had, so the argument would run, too much
evidence that the problems for every thinker are always
new ones offered by an intellectual milieu which is ever
changing. We may not suppose that there is more to be
learned from the *Meno* than how a great man thought in

his day. Our proper problem is why he thought so. Thus does one study steal its province from another.

These are the parallel positions: that Plato was constructing a Thucydidean history of what he considered the most important events which had ever occurred in thought; and that philosophy can be no more than a conjectural biography of an individual thinker. I have outlined them to suggest how wide is the range of the parable.

For us today all these questions are complicated by the dominance of scientific example over our conceptions of intellectual method. Mill's rules of induction still haunt us. They whisper in our ears about Agreement and Difference and Concomitant Variation. We feel that no conclusion drawn from study of *one* war could be valid for others. Amusing parallels there may be, which propagandists on both sides can exploit. But to get anywhere we would have to survey and classify enough wars, mark well the precise respects which were and were not the same, arrange our quantitative data and plot our graphs— self-evidently an impossible undertaking. So too the educator, if he is ruled by the same prepossessions, will feel that no study, however deep, of one instance of verbal confusion could lead anywhere without a vast comparative survey, extensive collections of examples, batteries of tests and a statistically sound handling of the outcomes—and that too is a patently impracticable programme. In neither case is any disparagement of scientific method intended. In both cases we have simply to admit that a problem not fitted for scientific treatment has been raised. The great danger, however, is that some may suppose—so high is the well-earned prestige of science—that problems which cannot be tackled in that way are not problems at all and cannot be tackled in any other. Fortunately we know better or no one, for example, would get married. Here again every instance is unique; but there is plenty to be learned—not by scientific induction, however—about it.

A practical method for improving interpretation (most human relationships would come within its scope) will not then use the techniques of science in the restricted sense which has been indicated. Nor can it rely on the single lucid example even though it is presented by a Plato. That needs another Plato to study it, if the full profit is to be derived. The programme fails for lack of Platos. Nor will case-history studies of utterances as socio-economico-political products help us much. We should, of course, encourage such compilations. They feed the scholars who make them. Long may they continue to do so. But do they add to our acumen in interpretation? Pushed almost unimaginably further they might tell us *why* something was said. Would that tell us *what it was*?

A prevalent modern view answers: 'Yes! The only way of finding out what is being said is by discovering its causes.'

I have called this 'a view'. But these words (as always in such topics) can state very different views. One of these is a cynical suggestion about motives: 'There is a motive of some sort behind every utterance, whether the utterer knows what it is or not; find the motive and that will tell you what the crime was.' Backed by Freudian, Marxian, or Propaganda Analysis assumptions, this view heavily discounts the notion that a man's *guiding* motive might be merely to present what he sees. That notion has been traditionally our Pole Star, the framework of our universe, the basis of our intellectual currency, the gold standard of discussion. If we have really been forced off it, we do desperately need to take whatever soundings might tell us where we are. For myself, I cannot say anything about this suggestion without assuming that it is false. It is a good example of a self-destructive view. If we accept it, any statement we make about it becomes but a move in a game of diddling people into serving some end which is

not the search for truth. And this is a fatal objection whatever may be our theory of 'truth' even though by ^{sw}The
truth^{sw} we should mean no more at bottom than whatever
body of views best conduces to the general good. That
conception of truth would leave our mental currency
sound. It would give us a general standard. We would
differ of course as to what belonged to that body. But in
discussing our differences we would be serving universal,
not sectional ends.

None the less, of course, our wishes do twist our views,
and most controversies may well be battles of wills rather
than of the doctrines they dress in. That is no new discovery, though recent writers on meaning have sometimes
seemed to think so. They have in fact worked up so much
suspicion and spread it so widely that the resort to reason
and principle which is necessary to co-existence is heavily
handicapped. If propaganda is taken as the fundamental
mode of speech, good faith, in brief, is blighted. In the
supposed interests of the consumer, the blighters can
easily destroy the crop.

There are deeper views which have to say also that
meanings are causes. But these views go so much deeper,
are so much more microscopic and abstract and exact, that
the 'meanings' and 'causes' they are talking about become
too different from those we have been discussing to come
in here. It might be true (as determinists of one sort
believe) that every human action depends upon everything that has happened in the universe. If so, every
human act, in that respect, would exemplify the same law
of universal dependence, but that would not in the least
be either what Thucydides maintained or what his
modern opponents deny. Here we have another example
of a perennial trouble in interpretation. Sometimes deeper
or more microscopic views are practically relevant to
operations on more everyday levels. Aerodynamics enter
into the design and handling of planes. But more often

there is no relevancy. The path of a ball exemplifies aero-dynamics but it would be absurd to make a study of aero-dynamics part of any player's training. Nor, I suppose, will the voter and the statesman interpret the better for too deep a penetration into the theory of the growth of meaning.

What we need is nothing so recondite, but a way of heightening our power to recognize what language— with its inevitable suppleness—is going to do to us in the next important thing it tries to say; some way of training ourselves to profit from our past experience with language more directly than through the wear and tear of the hither-ing and thithering of thought.

Traditionally, we have looked to logic to provide this. But there are as many sorts of 'logic' as there are sorts of 'history'. Any logical practice which assumes (as the syllogism for example must) that its terms have been made clear and fixed, increases, if anything, its student's capacity to mislead and to be misled. Modern symbolic logic spends its energy in trying to discover what it is itself doing and anyhow has gone apart to develop tech-nical languages of its own. These seem to have less than we hoped to teach us about the everyday languages we live by. The undertaking has made logicians more aware of the limits and the conditions of the logics; but the relevance of logical analysis to verbal conduct has not become more apparent. Improvement in its practice with language is what the world needs. How best can we aim at that?

How if we tried arranging series of statements wherein the same words change their meanings with their work. Suppose we put very obvious instances first, and followed them up with less and less obtrusive cases. Couldn't we then use such a scale of specimens of some one type of flexibility to develop skill with it—much as we use sums of progressively increasing difficulty to train skill in arithmetic; or graded examples of the use of the lever to train insight in mechanical principles? The sentences about history which open this essay, and their parallels, might stand near the advanced end of such a scale. Thucydides and the moderns, someone might say, are looking at 'history' from different points of view. But are they? Is what they are calling 'history' (their ˢʷhistoryˢʷ) at all the same thing? If they were talking about different things, both parties might be right. It is hard to allow this if one happens to be for the moment a partisan on either side. But it is much harder to hold the two interpretations of ʷhistoryʷ which make this possible, clearly and steadily in view together. There is a strain in doing so. Anyone who has learned to look at stereoscopic views without a stereoscope will feel that talk about 'seeing' and 'views' is no slight figure of speech here.

Understanding what Thucydides meant tends for the moment to incapacitate one for understanding what the moderns are saying, and *vice versa*. Each view tends to twist the other into something contradictory to itself, into something which is either a fatal objection or silly nonsense. This painful wobbling of the intellects is really remarkably like binocular rivalry. Both views grow bleary; they fade out till, with an almost audible click, there they are—combined and supporting one another in a perspective which requires just the very differences which were troubling us before.

To take a rather simpler example. A delegate at a Foreign Trade Convention will rise to ask: 'What is this much talked about Latin-American psychology? Don't all honest traders have the same psychology everywhere? I want to know what this psychology is?' Perhaps everyone in the convention hall feels more or less clearly that he sees what the gentleman is doing and what he is overlooking. Minds are alike, yes. They must be or they would not be minds. None the less, different customs, cultures, conditions . . . do divide us up into groups, and it is as true to say there are different psychologies as to say that human psychology is everywhere the same. Indeed these local differences are a necessary outcome of the universal sameness. The two seemingly opposed positions in fact fit together. But this will not, as a rule, prevent something of a wrangle from developing, though less heated reflection soon clears it up.

This is what happens when the examples are just difficult enough to stretch our wits. Commonly they are too difficult. Most of us have a suspicion that the great antinomies of the philosophies are too difficult and yet that if our wits were more nimble we would achieve a vision in which the rival doctrines all made sense together, in fact belonged to one another. And with the less abstruse controversies, the issues on which we vote or are polled, it is often the same. Only here, if we are candid, we will probably confess, each in the privacy of his self-scrutiny, we do not often enough make the peculiar effort needed and urge our wits to be nimble enough.

Very simple cases of the same types of sense change we commonly take so easily in our stride that we do not notice that changes are occurring. We allow for them automatically, unless we suspect that someone is setting us a trap. Thus the remark 'I read that book you told me about' causes no trouble in spite of the fact that two books —copies of the same book—were probably read. Compare the College Entrance Board Test argument of some years ago:

This book consists of small quantities of paper, thread and ink. Small quantities of paper, thread and ink have little value. This book is of little value.

This is a sense change of a different type from those we have been considering. Though fairly simple, experience shows that this example can trouble many. When we manage such simple changes easily the effect is frequently

86

that of pleasantry. When the Library at Yale was opened one of the speakers suggested as an inscription:

> This is not the Library;
> The Library is inside.

So might a Brazil nut be pictured as saying:

> I am not the nut;
> The nut is inside.[1]

In between the sense shifts which are too easy and too hard come those examples which can help us to interpret better if we arrange them in a mutually illuminating order. Thus the 'psychology' example may help with the 'history' problem.

The shift of the word 'history' is more complex. It combines in one movement three changes with which separately we are very familiar. One is the switch from an event to an account of or name for it—the switch we often indicate by one use of quotation marks. History is what happened. It is also men's accounts of this. It is this switch which has led historians sometimes to use the word 'historiography' to distinguish the account (especially as written) from what is recounted. It is odd that the *Shorter Oxford Dictionary* omits this last sense—'the events which form the subject matter of a history' as Webster puts it. This surely is the sense in which we should understand, for example, 'Happy is the country which has no history' —a country to which nothing happens, though people who are pleased to be ironical at the expense of historians may read it the other way.

The second switch is from a particular instance to the general character it exemplifies. The word 'word' illustrates it clearly. There may be 23 occurrences of ᵒᶜtheᵒᶜ

---

[1] I take my examples from Christine Gibson's *Words at Work,* a collection of interpretation exercises for classroom use put out in an experimental edition by Language Research Inc. Film strips of some of these exercises are in design.

on a page. Each is a separate word, they are 23 words. But the definite article 'the' is also one word. C. S. Pierce who analysed this at some length sometimes called the 23 words *tokens*, the one word a *type*. This switch is incessantly occurring. It came in our example about the book (books) the two men had read—as we would expect since a book is a system of words. Indeed without this switch it is doubtful if language would work.

The third switch is that to 'the pregnant use'—'He was a man!' said Hamlet. Hamlet senior was not merely human, but an example showing what man is in essence or idea. Most words will take this shift. 'Example' itself naturally does. So Thucydides' History becomes not merely an instance of historiography recounting instances of events in history, but *the example* through which we may see what must happen. It offers us a token not merely as a token, but as peculiarly representing the essentials of the type. A type, in Pierce's sense, cannot be presented in itself. No one can produce *the* word 'the'; it is tokens of it in speech and writing which can appear—in countless different forms. We suppose indeed that, to the ultra-microscope, no two will be alike. But that does not prevent some from displaying better than others what a 'the' should be to be a 'the'.

These three are components in the sense shift which causes our confusions over 'history'. Separately they do not often give us trouble unless something in the context makes us stumble. In conjunction they can make any mind wonder what it is thinking of.

This has been one way—a complicated way—of describing what happens. I have used a simpler account above: the modern view of history is a particularist view; Thucydides' a general one. Any man's life when seen in full biographical detail is unique. Seen in broad enough outline lives are alike enough to make insurance business possible. In countless discussions, understanding fails because one party is taking a particularist, the other a general view. Words cannot usually indicate the *scale* or *level* on which they are to be taken.

Is this a rival account of the shift of meaning of ʳhistoryʳ from which we started or an alternative formulation? Hold a moment! I am talking as though there was just a shift (complicated or simple) which is *the* shift of meaning in question. It is extremely hard not to talk so. And yet this obviously assumes a great deal. It assumes a very extensive sameness in our understandings of these two different senses (as we call them) of ᵒᶜhistoryᵒᶜ. Presumably all our understandings of either of them differ in some degree. But to talk at all of them we have to assume a sufficient likeness in a relevant respect. This we take for granted. We have to. I am not questioning the necessity we are under to stabilize meanings at some stage in this fashion if we are to converse at all. But we should realize that we are doing so, that we *are* taking common ground for granted. Only then can we avoid taking it for granted too soon. It is taking this for granted too soon which leads to futile verbal warfare, through the conviction that the other man must be denying something we see or believe to be true. The way I am suggesting to make such things more manageable is to study examples of simpler combinations of the shifts, passing through plane geometry, as it were, to conic sections.

We must beware, however, of letting analysis—of the sort which I have just been attempting—take the place of living examples. Graded series of quandaries in interpretation can be assembled only with the aid of some theoretical scaffolding. But it is not knowledge of the scaffolding, or skill in erecting it, but practice in interpretation which can help us. We may doubt if all the pages on metaphor ever written can make one man or woman a whit apter in its use. Enjoyment of good writing and good talk certainly can. But if so should we not expect that familiarity with good discussions will sharpen our discernment of these other shifts of word senses? To some degree no doubt it does; with this important difference. There is a strong inducement to understand good metaphors. In most discussion in which sides can be taken there are strong inducements to misunderstand. Discussion traditionally is verbal warfare. We may lose an immediate advantage by giving the other man's point a too sympathetic understanding. So exercise in familiarizing ourselves with these shifts of senses must be taken out of the arena, and since they are no more if no less alluring than practice in trigonometry (with no logarithms to help us) this means we must find room for them in the schoolroom. And that means in the training of teachers.

But this truly daunting topic requires a separate treatment.

VIII

Responsibilities in the Teaching of English[1]

A CONNECTED over-all view of the tasks, the methods, the norms, and the ends of English teaching—from the nursery school to the university, and from Bloomsbury to Yunnan—does not yet exist. Few ranges of human activity more deserve an encompassing, planetary regard; few receive less speculative attention. Yet no study more needs a radical questioning which would develop an explicit statement of what should be the directing implicit assumptions. The teacher of English, at whatever level, is oddly reluctant to discuss his principles. He takes them for granted. Whether they could be granted, were they available for inspection, must be doubted until they are set forth. This shyness may indicate the presence of beliefs too deep to be confessed. It may result, on the other hand, from a felt absence of any notion as to why, in any philosophic sense, he should be doing as he does—or be teaching English at all.

It is as a step towards a clearer, more continuous view of the wide range of endeavour which starts before the ABC and ends, say, with the English Tripos or the self-examinations of a visiting lecturer to China, that I venture to put these remarks together. Whether they commend themselves to others or not they may at least serve to

[1] This article appeared in *Essays and Studies by Members of the English Association, the 1947 Annual* (London: Oxford University Press).

focus reflection on certain points within an undercriticized field of possible design. My first remark, indeed, is just that English teaching is at present relatively planless. In comparison with modern teaching of mathematics, physics, biology, music, or even history, English teaching rarely asks, 'What should come before what?' with any insistent demand for a detailed, worked-out reply. The ideas which would govern the working-out of a reply are in fact not brought in. These are not recondite ideas, unusually complex or highly abstract. When active in other fields they are recognizably common sense. But in English studies—and increasingly as these become 'advanced'— they are tedious to apply. For this reason—and other, more respectable, reasons on which I will touch later— they have not been applied.

Examples are necessary here. I take them from very early stages of English teaching: beginning reading and the first stages of English for a student who comes to it as a second language. In these relatively simple first steps the needed conceptions of design, which are, I believe, commonly absent in English teaching, can be clearly made out. These instances can then serve as paradigms in examining more intricate later stages.

Before entering upon these details two remarks of wider scope may be in place. The first concerns the continuity of all stages in the learning of English (or any other language). Learning to read at the truly elementary stage of first seeing words as words, and learning to read—shall we say Shakespeare—too easily separate themselves in the teacher's mind. They are not separated in the learner's mind, however; the later stages are still in close organic connection with the earlier, and in countless ways. They are phases of one development, in which tricks, traits, habits, formed earlier continue to persist and display themselves through new material. Thus certain ways of guessing at words—regardless of their companions—

recur as ways of guessing at meanings—regardless again of their companions. And attendant incuriosities as to what went wrong and inabilities to consider this remain also. These continuities, however, are not a current concern of either the teacher of elementary reading or of Shakespeare. Both are more apt to blame 'native stupidity' or a low I.Q. than faulty method in teaching. And the teacher of Shakespeare may be surprised if one of his colleagues deserts Literature for a while in favour of illiteracy as a prime field of interest.

My other general remark is that two-thirds of us on this planet are, at the time of writing, analphabetics. Of the 2,200,000,000 people now breathing, some 1,500,000,000 either cannot read at all or read some non-alphabetic script. This is no time or place in which to argue the merits of the invention of alphabetic writing. Suffice it that if there is to be any truly world-wide communication between peoples within a foreseeable future, it will be in some language which is alphabetic. It could be within our lifetime and through English.

The technical problem of illiteracy, then, is the problem of making the initial phases of learning to read an alphabetic script as easy as possible. Current practice makes it far harder than it need be. Again, learning any second language is, by current methods, harder than it need be. In the case of English it has been many times harder. Experiment shows that a year of ordered English can give the beginner an entrance into the language hitherto rarely achieved in five. And with that a medium is available for truly world-wide communication and participation in planetary affairs. If parallel improvements were worked out in the ordering of higher level materials we could then develop what man so urgently needs: a common purpose jointly understood. And this is the only remedy powerful enough to protect him from his suicidal forces—a multiplication of his intelligence and a reformation of his will through an operative knowledge of what he can be and should be.

This greatest instauration indeed still requires the working out of parallel and more intricate improvements in the *order* in which materials at higher levels are put before the forming mind. The leap here made from the initial steps to the ends they serve—from *A First Reader* to Shakespeare—may seem over lofty. But the successes which order makes possible are highly encouraging. And —here is the point of these illustrations—this re-ordering would be governed by the same conceptions and be a continuation of the same reform.

Let us first see, then, in outline, how learning to read may be made easier—and *more instructive*—and how a first stage in English as a second language may be improved in design.

Whether reading should begin with sentences, or words, or syllables, or letters, is a question which has occasioned no little dispute. It is answered—and the dispute should be ended—when we perceive that reading may start with these all together, with sentences short, clear, and simple enough for the words, syllables, and letters which compose them to be studied *in* the sentences themselves. But to do this we must limit and control the letters with which these sentences are written. Twenty-six letters may seem few, but when they are all strangers and while the very notion of what a letter is, and does, has not yet been formed, and the trick of *seeing it* has not yet been learned, we shall do well to cut down the number of different letters used at the start to a minimum, adding to them, step by step, on a thought-out and tested plan.

With which letters, then, should our initial and early sentences be written? With those least liable to be mistaken one for another. The letters most liable to be mistaken are: symmetricals, *pb*, *qb*, *un*, *pq*, *db*; and letters which are more or less complete forms of other letters: *oce*, for example.

As with most mistakes, there are good biological reasons for mistaking *p* for *d*. It is the same thing in another position. It has been rotated on the plane of the paper. And *d* is the same thing as *b*—rotated on a plane perpendicular to the paper. It is highly important that we should see a common object, a knife say, as the same thing whatever its position or however it may be turned. A chief part of the difficulty of learning to read is precisely in unlearning (or better, suspending) this invaluable perceptive skill. It is hard to unlearn. Accountants are said to retain to the end of their days a liability, when fatigued, to mistake 6's for 9's.

Parallel considerations apply to letters which are incomplete forms of other letters. Perception is mainly a filling in of what is only in part presented. In selecting the letters with which to write the first sentences offered to a reader, the sentences through which he has to make the revolutionary *perceptual* adjustments required in learning to read, and the equally drastic *intellectual* adjustments enforced by the use of graphic symbols, these considerations should be taken seriously. The effect is to make possible a very great simplification of the beginning reader's task. Seven letters—liable to be confused only to a minimal degree—are enough for the composition of a sufficient supply of suitable short initial sentences. The problems of the management of the eyes can be mastered through sentences using but half the alphabet. The controlled introduction of the rest of the letters can then be managed so as to avoid the confusions mentioned. The learner's mind has been protected from the simultaneous impact of too many rival, unfamiliar, and mutually distracting opportunities for error.

This, indeed, is the key point which this illustration of teaching method applied in a simple field is designed to bring out. The subjection of the would-be learner's mind to too many confusable problems at once is the source of most intellectual and moral frustration. Unordered presentation, inadequately planned, forces upon him, in his attempts to learn, procedures which are *uninstructive*. He does not see what he is doing; and therefore, when the new, partially parallel task comes, his learning has not been built into him as a power of seeing what is required of him and how he can meet it.

The same moral—that customary modes of teaching expose the learner to (indeed plunge him in) an unnecessary and avoidable welter of misconceptions, often permanent—appears in my next illustration. Most beginners in English as a second language are exposed to a miscellany of words and structures which might be selected for the purpose of inviting confusion rather than avoiding it. To substantiate this serious charge needs a volume, and the presentation of a sequence of steps into English which seems most widely and deeply instructive to the learner takes another.[1] Only the principles of method which rule the order of such a sequence can be pointed out here. They are the same as the principles which should govern beginning reading. As there we selected a minimal initial set of letters, minimally confusable with one another, for the composing of our first body of materials, so here we select, for the start, a minimal set of words minimally confusable with one another in sense and syntactic function. With these we establish the first semi-mechanical operations—the grasp of simple English word order—as there we used less than half the alphabet in establishing good optical reading behaviour. Thenceforward we add vocabulary (and syntactic variants)—just as we added letters—with two principles in control: the postponement until it is safe of anything very liable to be mistaken for, and thereby to unsettle, what has already been learned;

[1] See *English Through Pictures* (Pocket Books Inc., New York).

and the maximum and most varied exercise of past gains in new tasks. The sequence in brief is *organic*—what follows depends on what has come before and in turn protects, confirms it, and illuminates it.

So abstract an account can mean little without the detail into which I must not enter here. The principles work out to a first stage of English sufficiently *instructive* to keep later advances in order, whatever their direction and however they are arranged. This first stage of English is, in other words, a comprehended structure strong enough, clear enough, and general enough to allow whatever further English the learner picks up to be attached to it—without the structure becoming *broken* or the accretions misplaced. In some ways this structure is analogous to a body of elementary mathematical knowledge incomplete, naturally, but supporting and controlling whatever ensues. It is *not*, however, theoretical knowledge: an affair of rules, but concrete skill: a body of understood practice.

This first stage of English can be surprisingly compact. It can be kept down to about 500 words. I say 'can' because learners so frequently add to it extras from outside the text or course that by the time you have taught it, it has become in the minds you are teaching a support for much more. Only in the artificial form of a text deliberately using nothing else can you separate it. In actual use it becomes, in the minds of learners with different interests, needs, and contacts, a central shared body, a common stem. As such there is no advantage in trying to specify this stage with more than perhaps 90 per cent particularity. A marginal flexibility is desirable.

Such a first stage of English is, from the principles which generate it, a partial use of Basic English, though it has no need for that exact minute specification, as a system, which Mr. Ogden, for his purposes and in consonance with his genius, gave to his invention. His work has in my opinion, been a historic and decisive step in the application of methodological intelligence to language teaching, a step which is already having beneficial effect almost throughout that field—and a step without which the design of such an organic introduction to English as I have been describing would have been impossible.

The setting forth of my second illustration has taken more space than I had hoped. Its place in the general argument rather than its detail is my concern here. At two elementary but important points in the teaching of English—points at which what happens and how it happens may affect, for good or ill, all that ensues—certain conceptions of method in the selection and ordering of what is taught can, I have tried to suggest, make a decisive difference to the prospect of success. I have said nothing about the time factor, though those who know how many illiterates give up because their progress is too slow, or those who will compute the wasted boy-girl hours now being spent in language learning, will not think this unimportant. I am influenced more by the change in *morale*, the reconstruction almost of personality in retarded children and illiterates who learn to read after years of defeat, or in the baffled student of English who suddenly finds himself able to use it. In both instances the effects can be of the very kind which apologists for the study of Literature customarily allege to be its peculiar benefits: a steadying of judgment, an enhancement of responsiveness and understanding, a heightened sympathy and self-control. How often can an experienced teacher honestly say that these are, in fact, evident outcomes of the study of poetry and philosophy? How truthfully can anyone affirm that students of the humanities are in general more excellent human beings than others?

These questions, I know well, are over-simple and perhaps unfair. I believe, none the less, that the discomfort they cause us has good grounds. Judged by standards we *still* know—though they may not rule examinations—English, as we teach it, does not do what it should. And even by the narrower examinable criteria, it does not make its students markedly and demonstrably better readers and writers, wider and abler communicators. We should be surprised if a student of mathematics, or of biology, or of history, were not found to be a better mathematician, biologist, or historian than one who had paid no attention to the subject. We are not surprised, alas, to find students of poetry or philosophy who show no resultant advantage in understanding or in judging either poems or views.

Is there not then something wrong in the conceptions of method which guide the teaching of English? Are we not repeating through the higher levels the same distracting, obstructive, and frustrating procedures which lead so often to such poor results down at the levels of beginning reading and beginning English? If we could reform our methods higher up, might we not expect comparable gains? Let us look more closely into the parallels.

Over-complexity was the chief fault I pointed to in the earlier levels—the presence of too many too easily confusable elements out of which the varying significant wholes were composed. In beginning reading the elements were the letters. In beginning English the elements were words and syntactic forms. By the time most schoolboys begin English as a second tongue the struggles of beginning to read are a thing of the past and forgotten. Reading has come to seem nearly as automatic a business as breathing. Few mistakes are made and the only vestiges (in the biological sense) of earlier confusion may be a tendency to blind guessing in bewildering situations where a better-taught reader will look to see what the problem is.

For students of Literature—whether poetry or philosophy—the elements are *meanings*. It is not unwise to use a notoriously uncontrollable word here. It may remind us concretely of the problems which face our students—who

99

do not benefit as they should from the Literature they read. As letters compose words and words compose sentences, so in turn now the meanings of sentences compose *works*—or should do.

This ratio, proportion, or scale of parallels should be taken with care. It repays care and it can be very misleading. Thus the beginning reader does not see letters first and then note that they form, in varying combinations, different words. He sees a blur; has a hunch about what it means; and, guided by such hoped-for meanings, many times confirmed or denied him, struggles slowly to vision of the words and of the letters in them. Similarly the beginner in English does not start by seeing English words. He sees configurations of letters. The meanings (and sounds) which will make them into English words are lacking. And for this reason these configurations themselves are, for a while, highly confusable and as hard to keep track of as the illiterate's letters, or as nonsense syllables—which, in fact, they still are. What makes them distinguishable comes to them best through use in graded sentences at work. As we all know only too well, if we attempt to take in too many different sentences together they blur one another. The exact relations between them are all important—as the phrase 'organic sequence' would suggest.

Stepping up now to the task of the student of Literature, he sees letters and words and syntactic forms aright,[1] or should do. What he has to learn to see are configurations of meanings. At first, in any reading which is truly worth while, any reading in which a mind is *learning how to behave itself*, we none of us see either the items in these configurations or the configurations themselves at all

---

[1] If my memories of scripts handed in for the English Tripos serve me, this is less than true. When higher level functions are under strain, lower level activities are liable to reveal their weaknesses. Hence perhaps many instances of the humbler sorts of 'misreading'.

clearly. The same interdependence of part and whole rules this process, but the opportunities for misinterpretation are more plentiful and insidious. Worse still, the checks of evident error are largely absent. The mistakes of illiterates and beginners in English can be made to stare them in the face. Some critics and philosophers have never in their lives had to confess their foolishness. The number of items of meaning is so great, the kinds so various, and the configurations they may enter so manifold, that it is easy for the resourceful mind to behave as though it were exempt from error.

Possibly, even probably, the difficulties of reading justly are increasing. Within a well-defined tradition the items and the patterns they enter are fewer and clearer than amid the frothy emulsion of hitherto immiscible cultures in which to-day we live and move and aspire to win some being. Our novel acquaintanceship with the untraditional past and with oddities of thought and feeling from other cultures is unrhythming, it may be, the heart of our mental and moral security. Perhaps some such fear has had a part in shaping the policy of scholarship which has seemed to seek a remedy in an ever wider survey and assembling of ever more minutely determined fact. Facts, properly documented, are comforting things in an age which does not know what it is doing or in what to put its faith. Probably, however, the influence of the successes of science has had more to do with this policy.

Facts are no true comforts until we know how to take them; and that is just our problem. They are further items in configurations which we have to learn to understand. This observation long ago gave us our saying about the wood and the trees. There is indeed something reminiscent of the Babes in the Wood in much contemporary scholarship. They wandered up and down and to and fro. They went everywhere but out of the wood and were found in the morning (there was a morning!) under a heap of leaves. The story says that pitying birds buried them so. This seems a pretty fancy. I find it more likely that they collected these leaves themselves and perished through unregulated interest in the variety of foliation.

In less legendary language we do not develop a mind by giving it more facts but by helping it to judge relevance. It is relevance which tells us which meanings belong with which, and in what configurations, for a valid interpretation. The way to strengthen the sense of relevance is by exercising it with simpler problems rather than by adding elaborations.

There is room here for sad misunderstandings. 'Simple problems' are not necessarily easy or vacuous or lacking in interest. Since the days in which *The Shorter Catechism* was believed to be good reading for children, the pendulum has swung far—farther in America than in England —and it is a sound complaint now that children's school books, in the United States at least, have recently been far too multifarious and trivial in content. They have been made so in the interests of quantity and rapidity of perusal, which pays the publisher and has been thought to promote 'good reading habits.' But the habits were merely optical and a mind which meets no problems worthy of it does not learn how to handle them when they come. The effects of this underloaded early reading are often perceptible throughout life. There is a widespread belief that if anything is 'hard reading' that must be the author's fault. Competition between magazines and a general harping on the obvious favour this illusion.

The content of all reading to which classroom time is given should be, at all stages, as hard as the readers can handle. 'If the book is easy it should be burnt for it cannot be educative', as Whitehead put it. But there are all sorts of ways of being hard. Which of them, graded aright, would be fruitful? In terms of what are these organic sequences to be contrived? How, in the general and unlimited domain of human interest—of thought itself—can anything be done parallel to ordering the letters or settling priorities in vocabulary and syntax patterns? An alphabet is a concrete thing, and lexicology and even grammar are familiar and explored studies, insipid with unanimity, in comparison with the discrimination and arrangement of ideas, forms, operations, modes of apprehension (call them what we may) that has to be undertaken here. In the elementary parts of mathematics and of the sciences and of the crafts—a few strictly limited segments of thinking, where activities with predetermined means and ends are developed—grading has to a large degree been accomplished. We do know roughly how to start a student and what to put before him next. But with more entire acts of mind—where feeling, direction of the will, and intellection come to terms and develop together—the task of ordering the steps through experiment with varying sequences seems blankly impossible. Descriptions seem inadequate to distinguish between the structures we should have to order.

Here certain lessons in patience and in humility as well as in courage and worthy ambition may be learned from science, daunting though science has become for the moment through its ill-balanced success. It can teach us that we do not open up such mysteries by straining the mind's eye or by cracking the mental sinews, but by developing and applying adequate methods. And my main point is that the necessary methods are already available—though in great need of development and application.

In part they are philosophic, though this will be a discouraging remark to those who, with some justice, see in contemporary philosophy little but semi-systematic mutual misunderstanding practised professionally. Paint that side of the picture as black as we please, it is still true that we now possess immense resources for distinguishing and comparing different structures in meaning. The devices may be over-specialized. They have grown out of the study—too often polemical—of the highest levels of abstract and comprehensive thinking. They are far from ready for use upon the earlier stages of the ascent to such levels. But, as techniques of analysis waiting for this very different application, they exist; and only experiment in this new application will make them over into what is needed.

The field for such experimentation is, of course, the classroom, which has not yet, in spite of Plato, received due recognition as the philosophic laboratory. It is the place of places in which to investigate not merely the individual peculiarities of misunderstanding but the general laws of comprehension, which are those of self-ordering and growth. What conceivings are dependent upon what former conceptions; which ideas (or more integral forms) prevent which, obstruct which, destroy which; which are most readily mistaken for which, to the distortion of the growing fabric; these are among the questions such an investigation must seek to approach. Answers to them will rightly be seen to be far off—as far as modern physics from Democritus, perhaps—but these inquiries would be cumulative in effect as no others have been. For any advance in them is an improvement in the instrument of inquiry.

We are accustomed to such improvement in what Mr. Conant has recently been calling the accumulative studies, to be contrasted somewhat ruefully with philosophy and poetry, which do not improve continually in technique or go on from where predecessors left off. It has happened, however, most triumphantly at junctures where diverse methods have crossed over or interbred. But junctures, alas, are themselves cumulative—in demands and in penalties if they are not met. We have come to the juncture of the Humanities with the Sciences and all the stormcones are up.

The Humanities, as the studies which make man

human, have somehow to keep his powers of mischief from undoing him. The dauntless old pun: '*Humanity*, the virtue, *humanity*, the race!' defines their role. Whether they can fulfil it is now our question—a burning question indeed and in a new sense. For the earth which held our homes is now a collective stake to which we are bound. For what infidelity or for what heresy? The fuel is being heaped up. If we cannot answer the final flames will.

This is not a political, it is a cultural crisis. The political crisis is a by-product. Its source is not economic, not geographic (geopolitic), not even governmental or administrative; it is philosophic, it is in the strain between unreconciled views of man and of how to seek and secure his good. But one side has learnt how to put its views into effect, while the other has not.

On the one side are those who see men as particles pushed about by external forces, and their desires, opinions, and beliefs as mechanisms which may be manipulated—in their interests or in the interests of the manipulators, it little matters which. On the other side are those who see a man, not as a thing but as a sovereign person—however poorly prepared to rule himself. And while the manipulators find in every development of mass psychology, every study of public opinion, every extension of communications, new power to their hands, the humanists are still busy wringing theirs. And yet, if they cannot rise to the responsibility the juncture puts upon them, who can?

Perhaps those in the sciences and in the humanities who are open to reciprocal influences can. It is only in and through education—at once more scientifically and more humanly conceived—that our remedy will be found. Religion, poetry, science, politics, in separation, do not have it. Only a recreated organon, the United Studies, can give it. The world needs that as much as it needs a world government. The parallels will bear pressing: how can a

United Studies admit Science without the liquidation of the traditional human being?

The answer, it seems, is: only by a cross-over, by learning from science how to make the humanities accumulative too. Thereby they would acquire a future as well as a past, a growth pattern as well as a tradition. The smiles or shudders with which many a modern humanist will greet such a remark show how far unscientific misapplications of mock-scientific procedures have clouded the picture. It need not be so. The teacher of English, who may have supposed that I have been forgetting him and his responsibilities through these last pages, should remember his *Republic* (531D) and recall what the task of dialectic (its prelude ended) was for Plato, and how constantly metaphors from genetics led his thought on the teacher's art (*Phaedrus*, 277; *Republic*, 495). But references to Plato, whose words I have been echoing, obviously enough I hope, at so many points, will only depress those educators who would ban the *Republic* lest its use in schools breed another Sparta. A teacher who would truly follow the tradition which stems therefrom will see that education has as yet barely begun, that it is crippled by failure to imagine what more it can do, that most of its practitioners are 'little bald-headed tinkers' still, and that most of its products are still ruined young by our malpractices. He will ask himself, not supinely but actively, whether the failure of non-accumulative studies to advance is not due to the hugger-mugger, promiscuous, leave-it-to-nature style in which the seeds of all things are being strewn over the would-be student's mind.

IX

The Idea of a University[1]

THE man who invented the university may well have been Plato. His School, the Academy, lasted, they say—with ups and downs, more downs than ups—longer than even the University of Paris has lasted, and in idea, if not in fact, may have been the pilot model. It kept, at least, its name. But what is a name? When I first taught in Peking there were twenty-six Universities there; now, I understand, there is only one, if it *is* that. But what—behind any name—is a University?

We have Plato's outline programme, blue-print for University studies in the *Republic*. It is so familiar that we may miss its main point. This inquiry into 'What is Justice?' comes down actually to an inquiry into 'What would a just man be?' and 'How could we produce him?' A just man (or woman) is one with all his or her bits and parts and talents and abilities in their right places, doing their own work and not getting in the way of one another. The book lays out *together* an account of the just man and an account of the just society, an organization chart for man and for society: on the ground that we can hardly have a truly just man without a just society to produce him or a just society without just men to guide and guard it.

It may freshen this up if we use 'sane' along with

[1] Notes of a speech given in the Eliot House Symposium, Harvard, March 11, 1953.

'just'. A just man is a sane man—nothing out of order or unbalanced about him. Similarly, a just society is one in which no faction, no pressure group, no self-interested power-seeker, can push the rest of the citizens around. In a just society all serve, not their own aggrandizement, but the commonwealth.

The University is to be the supreme organ in such a society for producing men and women able and fit to guide and guard it: to guard it from foreign enemies (insane states) and still more from its bosom enemies, self-promoting power-seekers. Plato knew all about civil war —that for him was the worst of all possible evils. The only man, he thinks, fit for high political office is the man whose only motive for holding it is the *knowledge* that, if he evades it, some worse qualified man will hold it in his place.

Now, just what does a University *do* to produce such men: capable of such knowledge and thereby fit and able to govern themselves and the state? Here is the recipe. Take the cream of the school crop, the hand-picked short-list, the most talented, liveliest, young men and women, the courageous, untiring learners, and give them a long and all-important course. A course in what? Here is the course description: 'They will take the arts and sciences they have been educated in at school and put them into connection, in a comprehensive *synoptic* view of their relations with one another and with what truly is' (*Republic*, 537).

Most people will want to ask three questions about this astonishing programme: 1. Has any University ever tried seriously and thoroughly to carry it out? 2. Just what would carrying it out be like? 3. If it could be and were carried out, what good would it do? Would it help produce the juster, saner persons we so badly need?

1. Institutions very commonly don't pursue the ideals they are founded on. How far have Confucianism, Bud-

dhism, Christianity—three other cultural institutions having aims comparable in scope to Plato's dream University—how far have these followed the ideals they were founded on? Very likely Plato's Academy (even in his lifetime as its Director) sought almost anything rather than the *synoptic* view. It is arguable that *his* Socrates (of whom we know so little apart from Plato), that model he set up of the ideal University teacher, has in fact only taught people how to trip one another up and catch one another out rather than how to understand one another and use that understanding co-operatively to the common advantage. It is to be feared that the Platonic dialogues and their progeny have spread chiefly the strategy and tactics of intellectual combat. While the original aim may have been to teach people not to fight but to *comprehend*. There is a deep difference between a dispute about the position of a business and an auditing of its accounts, between refuting a man and converting him; that is, giving him— permanently and with the consent of the whole of him— a more synoptic view. (We are becoming more and more terrified of other sorts of conversion as we come to know more and more about how they can be brought about.)

2. What would a course for educing this *synoptic* view be like? Would it be at all like any of the General Education programmes? I doubt it. I think these mix subjects in our minds, as you mix ingredients for a dish or a drink, rather than invite us to ask: 'What, deep down, has each subject to do with all the others?' and, as a result of this asking, require us to reconceive the WHOLE to which all subjects belong: to reconceive that whole and to reconceive the member studies also. How many whose main concern is with some branch of Science imagine that through taking a Humanities course they may have to reconceive the sciences? How many humanists taking a General Education science course see themselves reconceiving the nature of poetry, their own nature, their very selves, as

an outcome? The endeavour towards the synoptic view can be as radical in its consequences as that. For its attempt is not only 'to see all things in their relations with one another and with what truly is' but to create the organ of comprehending which can do that. 'The eye altering, alters all', said Blake. We get no synoptic view through any routine eye.

Let me give you a minute, gem-like, lucid sample of this process of opposition and reconcilement:

> One evening more than twenty years ago Dirac, who was in Goettingen working on his quantum theory of radiation, took me to task with characteristic gentleness.
> 'I understand that you are writing poetry as well as working at physics. I do not see how you can do both. In science one tries to say something that no one knew before in a way that everyone can understand. Whereas in poetry . . .'[1]

Let me fill out this superb aposiopesis (= I leave that to you): *In poetry one tries to say something which everyone knew before in a way which no one can understand.*

This I take to be (if suitably regarded) not quite what Dirac intended, but a saying profoundly and dazzlingly true: *true* in a breathtaking way, but only if and provided that one realizes that—along with the mathematical switch of *no one* with *everyone*—the meanings of *know* and of *understand* undergo deep, systematic corresponding changes. These changes can be studied. Their imaginative study is a sample—for physics and poetry—of that bringing of the subjects 'into connection, in a comprehensive *synoptic* view of their relations with one another and with what truly is' which Plato considered a University to be for.

3. What good would all this do? Suppose the subjects, the faculties (in the individual and in the University), the studies: History, Poetry, Theology, Logic, Govern-

---

[1] J. R. Oppenheimer, 'The Age of Science, 1900–1950', *Scientific American*, September 1950, p. 21.

ment, Biology, Ethics, Psychology, Physics . . .—re-
arrange them and subdivide them as you will; such *play*
with collocations of these potential oppositions and alliances is all the fun: 'Don't keep students at work by force
but by play' *(Republic,* 537)—suppose that these studies
came to understand one another so well that they could
give up their war?

Through how many centuries have Poetry, or Theology,
or Ethics, or Social Theory—backing up reverence for
custom, for received ideas, for the routine line—oppressed
and precluded Science? It could be so because hardly
anyone, through all that time, could see that Science was
a possible subject, which could be oppressed and precluded. Now that Science has triumphed (except in the
semi-secret corners of reactionary minds) is there a reverse
action in progress? Overt oppression is not needed. Covert
and unwitting stultification is enough: a drying up in the
Humanities, a withering away of creativeness, under the
eager breath of that scholarship which is an infiltration of
scientific practice. Dangerous thought for Academics this,
of course. It feels odd to suppose that the actual, incred-
ible, but everyday triumphs of methodical comparison
are sucking the lifeblood out of everything with which
man has endured and protested and endeavoured in the
past. But it would have felt odd in the dark ages to suppose
that methodical comparison was being precluded.

'In the destructive element immerse', as that butterfly
collector in *Lord Jim* recommends. What if we could treat
the whole struggle between the sciences, the humanities
and the rest with the very same procedures ('putting into
connection, in a comprehensive, synoptic, view') which,
in specialized applications, have given science its success?
Suppose, through such an enlargement of our intellectual
ambitions, this competition for the best brains, for the
big grants, for *lebensraum,* for position and for power
declined. Suppose all this were much reduced through

synoptic study of, through fair auditing of, the various accounts of 'their relations with one another and with what truly is'—what would we have then?

We would have *authority*: an authority which would have behind it *all* that man knows in *all* his modes of knowing and *all* that he would will to become through *all* his quests for being. It would be an authority which could wholly be respected and accepted, because it would represent the whole man, not any party or pressure group among his interests. All authority derives from the consent of those who acknowledge it. (Any other government rests on coercion merely, not authority. The fears are a faction only in our minds.) The authority which Plato's *synoptic* view would try to give us could gain our complete consent, could be wholly persuasive, because it would unify us.

Our minds are in analogy with the world struggle: facing towards two ways of reaching unity. One is the way of force, the conquest, *by any side*, of the others, with the dreadful surgery, the blinding and maiming of the spirit, the suppressions and precludings which ensue. The other way to unity is through the task Plato wished on his University, that University to which we can so well apply Socrates' words at the end of Book IX of the *Republic*: 'Its pattern is already there in heaven for him to see who so desires; and, seeing it, to make himself its citizen. No matter whether it exists anywhere or ever will, this and no other is his commonwealth.'

X

Toward a More Synoptic View[1]

LANGUAGE I take to be pre-eminently *the learnt activity* of man, and *learning* itself to be the chief current mode of evolution, of world advance. I am struck, accordingly, by the vigorous attempts which Language Theory (Scientific Linguistics) and Learning Theory (Scientific Behaviour Study) have recently been making to achieve something like AUTARCHY or independence or isolationism, and by their revolt against or withdrawal from most other studies (their breaking off of diplomatic relations). I take Philosophy to be most usefully the overall name nowadays of the diplomatic services between the studies. I think this attempt to break away, to secede, on the part of these new sciences, Linguistics and Behaviour, is dangerous *for them* and *for others*. Both dream at times of intellectual world-conquest. Linguistic Science and the study of Behaviour alike have a certain young ruthlessness and regardlessness.

I am using this grand analogy (which is Plato's) between the not-at-all Universal Studies and the not-at-all United Nations to explain why in what follows I am

[1] In part from a talk given at the Eighth Conference on Cybernetics held under the auspices of the Josiah Macy Jr. Foundation in New York on March 15, 1951. A transcription of the discussion was printed in *Cybernetics, Transactions of the Eighth Conference*, March 15–16, 1951, 'Communication between Men: Meaning of Language'.

concerned with diplomatic-philosophic STRATEGY for the further study of language rather than with any specific investigation of any part or any attempted over-all picture. Perhaps the only other grand analogy which has had any comparable role is that to which this group here has recently given such impressive development: the organism-machine analogy.

Let me begin with a doubt, a pervasive and penetrating doubt—truly a bosom doubt. It concerns the language to use in these or any other remarks about language.

The very instruments we use if we try to say anything which is not trivial about language embody in themselves the very problems we hope to use them to explore. The doubt comes up, therefore: how far can we hope to be understood—or even to understand ourselves—as we use such words? And in the lucidity of this doubt the literature of this subject can take on a queer appearance. Must confidence be in inverse ratio to the security of its grounds?

This situation is not, of course, peculiar to the study of language. All studies suffer from and thrive through this. The properties of the instruments or apparatus employed enter into, contribute to, belong with and confine the scope of the investigation.

I can perhaps best put this more or less uncomfortable though familiar point and show its relevance to the strategic problem: How may the study of language be advanced? by using a quotation from J. R. Oppenheimer (*Scientific American*, September 1950, p. 22), his formulation of Bohr's *principle of complementarity*:

The basic finding was that in the atomic world it is not possible to describe the atomic system under investigation in abstraction from the apparatus used for the investigation by a single, unique objective model. Rather, a variety of models, each corresponding to a possible experimental arrangement and all required for a complete description of possible physical experience, stand in a complementary relation to one another, in that the actual realization of any one model excludes the realization of others, yet each is a necessary part of the complete description of experience in the atomic world.

It is . . . not yet fully clear how characteristically or how frequently we shall meet instances . . . in other fields, above all in the study of biological, psychological and cultural problems.

It may be worth speculating for a few moments on the sequence in which recognition of some such principle of *Instrumental Dependence* as this has struck the various studies as necessary.

Mathematics, I conjecture (but I speak of mathematics with a lively sense of my ignorance in such a company as this), may have been the earliest study forced to ask itself about its intellectual instruments.

The simpler the properties of the instruments the easier it may be to take account of them. If so, we might get some such sequence as this: Mathematics, Physics, Chemistry, Biology, Sociology, Psychology, Anthropology, Poetics, Dialectic. The parallelism of this sequence to the scale of increasing complexity of subject and to cosmic history or evolution would be not accidental. Furthermore, it might be held, the higher up you go on the scale of complexity, the MORE of the mind you bring in as apparatus or instrument of the inquiry. A mathematician, as mathematician, uses one branch only (though a prodigious branch) of human ability; the anthropologist has to be more many-sided, the student of poetics (I venture to say) more complete still.

Corresponding to all these studies are characteristic uses of language. Poetics, I suggest, is faced by the most complex of them. Above Poetics I would put only Dialectic as being concerned with the relations of Poetics with all the other studies and with their relations to one another. Dialectics would thus be the supreme study, with Philosophy as its Diplomatic Agent. All of them are *both* subject matter and language studies. That is the chief point here: there is no study which is not a language study, concerned with the speculative instruments it employs.

Let me linger a moment with Anthropology because of the close ties and great influence it has recently been having with Linguistics. Its chief methodological problem is, I think, almost exactly paralleled in Linguistics, though perhaps Linguistics—by somewhat drastic restrictions it has been putting on its scope, by concentrating on morphology, for example, and by what sometimes looks like a panic-stricken avoidance of semantic problems[1]—has been making better progress. This chief methodological problem I can put compactly with a quotation from A. L. Kroeber, 'Anthropology', *Scientific American*, September 1950, pp. 87–94:

> Anthropologists now agree that each culture must be examined in terms of its own structure and values, instead of being rated by the standards of some other civilization exalted as absolute—which in practice of course is always our own civilization. This principle leads, it is true, to a relativistic or pluralistic philosophy—to a belief in many values rather than a simple value system. But why not, if the facts so demand?

This 'basic principle of the relativistic approach' is fairly plainly a half-way house not permanently tenable. It would be better to say: an early *staging place* not nearly half-way—perhaps only a millionth part of the way, if you can imagine this metaphoric distance being metaphorically measured. It is a negative defensive step, an anti-imperialist move, necessary and desirable, of course, but not at all a sufficient principle for an over-all *comparative* study. It is parallel to the linguistic principle that the structure of a language is not to be described in terms of the structure of some other language (English grammar in terms of Latin, or Hopi in terms of English).

[1] This is out of date already. Meaning looks like becoming again *the* prime concern of Linguistics (1954).

What the linguistic scientists have been doing is fashioning a growing system of *instruments for comparing*: instruments able to put diverse languages into a common frame. They are not, of course, attempting to examine and describe Hopi in Hopi or Kwakiutle in Kwakiutle. They are working out over-all apparatus which can be, they hope, used for the examination and description of all languages. It may well be that any one such apparatus will for ever be unable to describe every feature of language. A ⌐complementarity⌐ situation may very well arise. But the apparatus hitherto devised keeps within narrow limits as to *which* of the features and functions of languages it is as yet ready to give an account of.

. . . The linguist focusses his attention upon those selected aspects of language which, he believes, his methodological equipment gives him the authority to investigate. He does not attempt to study the totality of language phenomena. (Stanley S. Newman, 'Behavior Patterns in Linguistic Structure', in *Language, Culture and Personality*, p. 94.)

The sharp separation which exists between linguistics and other disciplines is, at best, an arbitrary one based on the development of an isolated methodology and not on any empirical division of subject matter. (*Ibid.*, p. 95.)

This brings me back to the marked 'Ishmaelite Complex' so many 'linguistic scientists' seem to have suffered from. Their hand has been against all men—except only a brother linguistic scientist. I don't say 'and all men's hands are against them', but *they* seem to have thought so. Above all, their hand has been against all who like to think about language with instruments other than their own.

In part this is explained by the difficult labour they have had in working out their comparative apparatus even for selected and limited aspects. But the hostility and even contempt frequently shown for those who enjoy reflecting about meanings and the disdainful snorts they still emit against 'mentalism' need rather more accounting for. They share these things with some students of Behaviour who are also attempting to expand an isolated autonomous methodology. I think there has been some academic or at least intellectual persecution in both instances, though in both instances, I would think, that is over. The boots may now be on other legs.

It would be amusing if the attitudes of young sciences to their elders came to provide instructive case-histories for students of personality structure. The psycho-politics and psycho-therapy of Educational, Scientific, and Cultural Relations would make a nice new sub-subject, would it not? Juvenile revolt in young studies has its very good points, of course. It impels the growing study sometimes to invaluable ingenuity and agility in finding ways of not *seeming* to be doing or saying what the parent studies have been recommending as reasonable for some time.

There may be a good omen in this flight of fancy. I am perhaps somewhat influenced towards this frivolity by the trivial fact that the book I wrote with Ogden (a third of a century ago it is now) has been about equally attacked for being 'mentalistic' (J. R. Kantor, *An Objective Psychology of Grammar*, p. 66, for example) and for being 'behaviouristic' (Max Black—whom I mention because I wish so much that he were here). I have come back, you see, to my initial bosom doubt: What shall language about language be like? And typically, should it be 'mentalistic' or 'behaviouristic'?

I had better at once calm your worst fears by saying that I do not propose to solve this problem in this paper. I only hope to refrain, if I can, either from dismissing it or from assuming any answer to it—unless some analogue to Bohr's Principle of Complementarity would be an answer, or rather, a *staging place*.

To come at last to Circular and Feedback Mechanisms. And in what I am going to try to say now I am in considerable accord, I think, with Norbert Wiener (for example, his *Human Use of Human Beings*, pp. 73–84, on 'Rigidity and Learning') so far as the different conceptual and linguistic apparatus I can use permits me.

If the properties of the apparatus employed DO enter into, belong with, and confine the scope of the investigation, the problems I attempt to explore will be in certain respects *different* from his. How different is the accompanying methodological problem.

I am, of course, exemplifying (I would fain say illustrating) circular and feedback processes all the time (as we none of us can help doing in all our talk). I need not stay here to insist that in most modes of discourse what we say next (and how we say it) will be in part controlled by feedback (outcome reports) from what we have said already. (And let ᵂSAYᵂ here range as widely as you will.)

May I now *prepare* you to be receptive to, to expect and attend to, something which does not (I am often surprised to note) get so much space nowadays in discussions and publications on these themes as it used to? Perhaps it is considered by those who study feedback philosophically as included in some ingenious way under that term.

It stands, however, in a certain obvious, if superficial, opposition to that word and, in certain frames of thought, it will be given almost if not quite as much importance—sometimes even, in some connections, more importance—than feedback itself. And it is certainly as circular.

Have you, I wonder, fed-forward enough to know perfectly well that I am going to talk a bit about *feedforward*? Throughout the process of learning and using language (and at all levels, I think) feed-forward seems to be indispensable.

But before developing that theme a little, perhaps I should point to some instances of feed-forward at prelinguistic behaviour levels.

Most natural behaviour (as distinguished from some

artificially isolated behaviour—in some learning-theory experiments, for example) shows feed-forward. All activity (ACT-EEV-ITY, I'd like to say, putting a vocal tag on the word to show that it's here being used technically with a certain definition behind it. Scots have a reputation—which may be excessive—of knowing what they mean. And it is G. F. Stout's account of activity that I am using)—all acteevity depends on, and is made into acteevity by, feed-forward.

Take looking for something, hunting, searching, for example. We do not *find* anything unless we *know* in some sense what we are looking for. Nor do our humblest cousins among the animals. (I'd like, here again, to put vocal tags on *find* and *know*. They are correlative terms here. We may happen on something but we don't *find* it unless we are looking for it. *Finding* is the end-phase—in both main senses of ᵂendᵂ—to the acteevity of searching. Something is fed forward by coincidence with which that acteevity reaches its terminus and goal.)

Know, of course, in the sentence I've used needs very leery handling. It needn't, and in most cases shouldn't, mean more than just this feed-forward. Nothing need be implied as to how it is done—by an image of what is sought, for example, or by something much more generic or symbolic.

I know, I think, generically the grave doubts—to put it mildly—which some of you are feeling now. And my knowing them has been and will be a guide to my search for ways of meeting them. Focus your doubts and apply them, if you will, to the following example.

In my pocket are some pennies and a dime. I am going to find the dime by touch and partly by hearing: by the feel and sound of my finger-nail scraping on the milled edge of the dime. Something is being fed into my search (and into your observation of my search) which will, when the search reaches its END, tell the acteevity that it is successful.

Very probably some of you will have been saying to yourselves that talk about 'feed-forward' is just falsifying metaphor and that there is nothing here but TAPING (as with the instructions given on tape to a computation engine before it is set to work)—for a special run of mani-pulative-perceptual mechanism, plus resort to a memory store, plus *feedback*. And that the same holds good for all cases of so-called acteevity at all levels.

If so, that transforms the question into one about *taping*, about the sources of *ad hoc* tapings in organisms and their dependence on more general tapings. Tapings seem to be hierarchic, or to form an enclosure series—the widest, most inclusive or over-all tapings being least determinate. These feed forward, for their own mainten-ance and performance—guide and protect themselves by feeding forward—subordinate, narrower, more specific instrumental tapings and these do the same again and so on. . . .

For example, consider an animal hunting. There is a general very inclusive taping: 'Search for food!' As he scents this or that possible source, subordinate tapings are issued. Say he is a grizzly who scents ants. If the ants are under a boulder, in comes a sub-subordinate set of *ad hoc* tapings based on the shape and size and weight of the boulder . . . and so on. When he gets to the ants con-sumatory behaviour which has been fed forward puts an end to that sequence. Then perhaps the scent of some berries starts off a new round.

This is familiar line of speculation. What I hope it will help me to say is this: Feed-forward, for me, names the peculiar character of tapings which arise in the service of more generic, more inclusive, tapings. And, as such, the adequacy of any description or *valuation* of any acteevity depends upon recognition of the sources of its feed-forward. (But, lest ˢʷsourcesˢʷ should be taken here too lightly, I would put behind it what is said of and with ʳsourceʳ in Piece II. The wheel diagram there proposed is a device for imagining the dimensions, or respects, of *any* acteevity.)

Leaving now these teleological heights, or depths, let me briefly apply this sketch to language in action.

This is perhaps the moment to let my two major professional preoccupations out for a brief airing. I am by profession (1) a critic, (2) a pedagogue, especially concerned with teaching beginning Reading and with the early stages of teaching a second language. Criticism and pedagogy thus for me constitute two fairly high-level feed-forward systems tending and guiding two extensive worlds of relatively specific acteevity. And in both, though in different ways, *design*—a flexible fitting of means to ends—is nearly everything.

In Criticism, radically a valuative acteevity, the difference between better and worse utterances is in design. Poor speech and writing is poor either because it is not attempting anything worth trying or because it is inefficient. (The design, mind you, may be, and most commonly is, unwitting.)

This Principle of Efficiency is, I think, little more than a recognition of the enclosure series I have just mentioned, the hierarchical service: the *ad hoc* taping serving the wider aim which serves the wider, wider still, and the widest aim. . . . And since language is inescapably a social acteevity which only comes into existence with, and owes its whole character to, mutualities among men and within communities, the study of language, even in the most elementary stages, has to be a dependant of that highest generic taping which may be called ethics. It is concerned—endlessly—with standards and validity. It must be as *normative* through and through as, for example, the study of *medicine*.

How many other studies also must be? Must all? Medicine must be. But how about Biology as a whole? Is not that *Normative* in the sense that of each organism studied the student asks: 'How far is this a good, typical (i.e. normal) specimen?' Even of a disease we have 'a beautiful case'—one which is serviceable for feed-forward.

> We call, for we see and feel, the swan and the dove both beautiful. . . . Absurd would it be to make a comparison between their separate claims to beauty from any abstract rule common to both, without reference to the life and being of the animals themselves . . . or on any ground indeed save that of their own inappropriateness to their own end and being, their want of significance as symbol and physiognomy. (Raysor: *Coleridge's Sh. Crit. I*, p. 196.)

Here we have the anthropologist's 'relativistic approach' back again—in the service, this time, of aesthetics. But I am inclined to suggest that all studies whatsoever are normative in this sense by the very fact that their statements only work through agreements among users—*ad hoc* mutual and self-tapings—to use them so and not otherwise. In so far as someone does not so use them the over-all taping—the purpose of the discussion—is not (normally) served.

There are, of course, any number of inquiries—in linguistics as in every other study—which look, and will be strenuously maintained to be, *non-normative*. But still there are over-all questions for every such inquiry which are normative: (1) What is this for? (2) What is its bearing on other inquiries? (3) Are the conditions which generate and control the inquiry being observed? These put them within wider acteevities wherein they are judged—factually, yes, but more than factually too. (Indeed, as regards any or all of the respects which a Theory of Comprehending may choose to distinguish, see Piece II.)

Naive scientism with its autarchic policies can be a threat to us all here. There are vast areas of so-called 'purely descriptive' linguistics which are a grim danger at present to the conduct of language (see Piece I), to education, to standards of intelligence, to the reserves in theory and in sensibility of the mental tester: the danger is the worse for the keys to opportunity being so often in incompetent hands. The appeal to mere *usage*: 'If it's widely in use, it's O.K.', is a case in point. Every useful feature of language was *not in use* once upon a time. Every degradation of language too starts somewhere. Behind usage is the question of efficiency. (See *Interpretation in Teaching*, ch. xv and xvi.) Inefficient language features are not O.K., however widespread their use. Of course, to the linguistic botanist it is important to preserve all varieties until they have been collected and described. But that is not the point of view of the over-all study of language, its services and its powers. That over-all view is, I am insisting, inescapably NORMATIVE. It is concerned (as every speaker and every listener is always concerned) with the maintenance and improvement of the use of language. And for this reason, the 'scientific objectivity' of which many a linguistic scientist is so charmingly vain (like the boy with his first bicycle) is out of place when it tries (as it does) to interfere with education or criticism.

No doubt the job of 'collecting and arranging the facts of speech' has been much interfered with by silly normative prejudices in the past. Linguistics and medicine may be expected to develop analogous fads and quackeries. But that does not excuse retaliatory aggression. Here then is a place where philosophy, the diplomatic agency of dialectic, must intervene. It has to *protect* studies from the interferences of other studies, yes. But it has more to do. It has also to help studies out of *self*-frustrations due to their ignorance of what other studies can and should do for them.

A Synoptic View therefore—truly Universal Study— would have more than police functions; it should be advisor-general and therapist as well. And yet what exquisite discretion it would have to employ if it were not to impair the due freedom for growth in the autonomous studies!

On the other hand, an extended Complementarity Principle would amount to no slight Charter of Tolerance. Indeed some may fear it as a beginning of anarchy. Such high organization is a long way off, however; and it will be better to consider what steps might be taken toward it.

Let us remind ourselves once more that it is not a 'theory' or 'doctrine' we are in search of but a development of comprehending. I am shutting ˢʷdoctrineˢʷ in too narrowly in this remark: making it too merely a chain of statements (all 1, 2, 6, and 7: Piece II) and neglecting the *wholeness*, the mutuality of control among the dimensions or respects which has been characteristic of so much teaching. I did so deliberately because this very question: 'Do the structures of the typical utterances of different studies differ?' is perhaps a good one to set out from. By ʳstructuresʳ we should mean here ˢʷconnections between the various respects active in the comprehendingˢʷ. Mere difference in subject matter would be, in most cases, far less important: a difference in 1 chiefly and derivatively in 2. But differences in Selecting can speak for much more, all the way round to deep divergence of Purposing. They need not, of course; but it is when they do that the real difficulties of approaching a Synoptic View confront us. It is then, for example, that the religious and the scientific, the poetic and the ethical consciences can divide the mind.

Once again, it is not an *account* only of these difficulties which we need but a way of meeting and accepting them. And the chief use of an account might be as an aid to our honesty in judging whether we were or were not facing them. The cultures of the world offer us a wonderful display of man's capacities for self-deception:

> The gigantic anthropological circus riotously
> Holds open all its booths

but a few hours of any self-observant person's life can provide almost as rich and a nearer demonstration. How to be? How to reconcile the possible modes of being? That is no theoretical question but the choice of choices.

It may seem odd to equate *this* with the reconciliation of the warring studies and to take the faculties of the mind and the Faculties of a University into a serious pun together. It may seem odder, perhaps, some day not to do so. For the knowledges, though the gaps between them have been widening, interfere with people's modes of living ever more deeply. Indian, Chinese, American, English . . . we take what a College can give us as serviceable guidance today in far more than professional affairs. This is part of that transition from culture to education which Piece V touched on. It is a perilous transition, no doubt, but hardly new or, on our ordinary time-scale, sudden. If Mr. Eric Havelock is right, Socrates was put to death for trying to replace apprenticeship—association with and imitation of the knowledgeable—by instruction, and it looks as though the founding of the Academy itself was an early and decisive step in an interminable and necessary process.

Section Two

XI

General Education in the Humanities[1]

ONCE upon a time, somewhere, perhaps, when our forefathers lived in simple tribal societies, a man could get a good general education through docile acceptance of the current ideas. It is not so now. Any man, today, has to fight for his moral life to get one. And the hardest part of the fight is the effort to go on asking what a general education is, what is the good of it and what it is for.

No one can tell us what it is—in so many words. The words mean little or nothing unless somehow we know already what they would say. The answers have to be about what man is, what he may be and what he should be. We do not learn these things from short statements, however well they are phrased, or from long treatises, however persuasive. How can we learn them then? This is exactly our first question, 'What is a general education?' over again.

One way of learning them might be through familiarity with the best that has been thought and felt by the greatest minds of the past. And it seems sensible to start with the earliest of these. If Poetry, Religion, and Philosophy are the main confluents of the traditional Western

[1] A talk given in connection with the Harvard General Education programme and in explanation of a course on 'Sources of our Common Thought'.

human being, if they are the chief tributaries of the river in which we, as individuals, are little whirls or eddies, then a knowledge of their headwaters should help. Homer, the Old Testament, and Plato are these headwaters. These ancient authors in a sometimes distressing fashion are authors of more than books. They made and make *us* up —whether we know it or like it or not. They are the founding fathers of our tradition, and guide even our attempts to be rid of it.

So put, this can be an alarming thought. Freud has taught us to be uneasy about paternal influences. We may well wonder how long—on through the millions of years which (until nuclear physics dawned) lay before Western civilized man—how long are these Big B.C. Three to rule him? 'Origins are inescapable' is a formula which will bear a great deal of interpretation. Our questioning of it in particular instances makes up most of general education: the inquiry into the hierarchy of the questions, *or* which questions should come before which?

The first great questioners seem to us, too often, to be *answerers*. That is our fault. We misread them, forgetting that no man says anything new and important unless under the urge, or after the tension, of questions. Homer may at first sight seem an exception; but what is Achilles but a question? Do not ask me what it is. The only way to know it is to know the *Iliad*.

When one knows it, one comes to doubt that easy opening sentence I began with. Homer is tribal education at its height. Perhaps all education is questioning and good education is simply ordered questioning leading to what we—with planet-dwellers' indifference—are equally willing to call the highest or the deepest questions?

Knowing and questioning, of course, require one another. We understand nothing except in so far as we understand the questions behind it—and that is never very far. Near the close of Canto IV of *Paradise*:

130

. . . Our intellect is never satisfied unless the Truth illume it,
beyond which nothing true extends. In that it reposes, as a wild
beast in his lair, so soon as it has reached it: and it can reach it;
otherwise every desire would be in vain. Because of this, doubt
springs up like a shoot, at the foot of the truth; and it is nature
which urges us to the summit from height to height.

Short of that summit, truth from which no doubts spring up is
dead.

The Old Testament—as soon as we begin to see what
comes before what among its writings of a thousand years
—is an unparalleled exhibition of titanic questionings
followed by wooden-minded formalism and miscompre-
hension. It enacts before us, on the grandest scale, the
perpetual human tragedy—the transformation of originative inspiration into the neat note and devout observance
of the make-the-grade examinee.

Thus the Old Testament can present to us—against
an appropriate background of fears and thunders—what
general education is *not*, together with much to suggest
what it might be. Plato too—without the fears and in
what feels like perfect spring weather, though historians
know better—shows us two sides. Some will tell us that
the source there of general education is Socrates—shining
through an increasing haze of Plato's 'dear gorgeous nonsense', as Coleridge called it. It seems more likely that
both must share the praise, as well as the blame, of inventing the art which is still man's best hope and worst bane
—the art of conscious controlled interrogation which
turns so fatally into a technique of purblind disputation. Here again something which is not general education
displaces how much which suggests what it might
be.

To the end—wherever the pursuit leads us—we gain
general education only by asking what it is. But we cannot
ask such a question in the void. It does no good to interro-
gate merely the words *General Education*. We must have

materials—samples to examine—while remembering that it is our business to be examiners, not examinees. We must not let the routines and mechanics of the learning-teaching trade get in the way. We must not forget that it is *samples* we are examining. Samples of what quality? Samples of what?

The question is general education at work again.

February 1947.

XII

Queries[1]

M AY I call what I'm going to offer you: 'Theory of Querying' and ask first: 'What is a Query?'?
And then go on to contrast with it: 'What is a Theory?'?

Will you forgive me, incidentally, for not putting this all into rime?
Theory . . . Query—not too promising a start maybe?

Why do I take Queries first?
Wouldn't it be more natural to start with a *definition* of a Theory (or Proposition or Statement), or at least some sort of indication of what a Theory is, and then from that go on to describe or define a Query?
We'll agree, I take it, that *is* the usual plan? That, as a rule Questions are taken to be in some way derivative from or dependent upon Statements? That Questioning is a special attitude we may or may not take up toward Statements?

But why should we make Queries thus parasitic upon Theories?
Doesn't the converse really make better sense?

[1] Some remarks made at a meeting of the Philosophy Department, Harvard, in October 1945.

Don't questions really come before answers, phylogenitic-
ally, ontogenetically, psychologically, logically, historic-
ally, and even philosophically?

If so, wouldn't it be better to try to give an account of
questioning first and then see if we can't describe *assertion*,
statement (even the bare *entertaining of a proposition*) in
terms of the querying activity? As, for example, a sort of
precipitate from it: a deposit, a sediment, an opaque sub-
stance, in brief, a MUD,

thrown down by

the clear

translucent

lucid

fluid

medium of

thinking?

Do some of you, or all of you, already detect something
BIASS'D

—and ∴ to be suspected?—

in the way I am putting these Queries?

Have I made any statement yet?

   They are all Queries, aren't they?

Might it not be a mistake in strategy from the outset to
develop an Inquiry into Querying through anything but
Queries?

If there is a bias in the attitude to Queries I'm displaying
isn't that as it should be?

In an incomplete provisional Inquiry
—and all but God's are such I take it?—
isn't 'bias' necessary?

Isn't calling this 'bias' just a pejorative turn—suggesting
that some other direction would be more to our taste?

Does a question have to have a direction?

134

Can't it go all ways at once?

Doesn't a question have to have a direction?

Can it go all ways at once?

What will you make of the differences between these two ways of asking?

Does the frankness of the metaphor here distress you?

Is it more distressing than the other uses of the same sort of metaphor which depict propositions as the starting-out points, or terms, or goals, etc. of questionings?

And is calling a Query a *motion* (or *process*, or *vector*), is that strictly a ˢʷmetaphorˢʷ?

But to come back—does it make any important difference whether we take questioning or assertion to be primordial —and the other derivative?

Well, what sorts of differences would we regard as important?

If the switch over let us or made us see traditional doctrines and data from a new angle would that be important?

If it gave us different ways of formulating

—ought I to say *them*, or call them their 'Query-analogues'?—

would that be important?

If it suggested new questions, would that be important?

—Or have we more than enough questions already?—

On a humbler level, if the switch were *pedagogically stimulating*

—ghastly words both of them, aren't they?—

would *that* be important?

Penultimately, have we any means of inquiring, with any hope of valid results, into the questioning process?

   (Where—in the formulation of any question comes the

Whatever-It-Is which formulates and propounds and asks it?)

And what would valid results be?

    Other Queries?

Finally what has philosophy to show but Queries:

    What is Being?

    What is Thought?

    What is a Proposition?

    What is Logic?

    What is Philosophy itself?

    What is Man?

    What is God?

as the outcomes of its agelong endeavours?

XIII

Language and Value[1]

M
Y title would let us discuss almost anything. However, I propose to narrow my topic down to:

'Some reflections on the source of Value and on
Language as our chief exerciser of Choice.'

I hope (not very hopefully) we may agree that the most
important points in this discussion are best regarded as
affairs of CHOICE, not of FACT.

May I invite you—to begin with—to linger more than
a moment over this distinction:

matters of choice,

matters of fact.

I am going to suggest that this distinction may have a
lot to do with two questions this Group has been discussing in recent meetings:

(A) On what can be based a universally acceptable
ideology?

(B) How can we find an ideology that will motivate
moral behaviour?

(These questions sound rather differently in Boston
and in Benares.)

I have some doubts—by the way—whether an 'ideol-

[1] Notes for a talk to the Science and Values Study Group of the Insti-
tute for the Unity of Science, American Academy of Arts and Sciences,
April 10, 1952.

ogy' (in any of the recognized senses) is either what we want or what men need, and—to anticipate—I wonder how much of what *we* are likely to consider *moral* behaviour would go on being considered *moral* in a UNIVERSALLY accepted scheme of conduct.

Matters of FACT; matters of CHOICE: this is not perhaps a very clear distinction—at least in many possible examples it isn't. Sometimes it may seem brilliantly clear:

If I ask a man who is about to take a photograph, 'Are you using colour film or black and white?' the chances are very good that he will reply in terms of FACT—according to his memory of what he put into his camera.

On the other hand, if I ask him, '*Would* you use colour film or black and white?' the chances are fairly good that he will reply in terms of CHOICE—a certain subject, light and purpose being in view.

The use of 'would'—combining a volitional with a future conditional meaning—is an invitation to him to do so.

But very likely he will go on to give reasons for his choice, to offer arguments in its favour; and these may come to hide the affair of choice they were used to justify. They may make it look like an affair of fact: a causal conditional.

Still the distinction, in such an example, may, I think, be kept clear.

But take a more complex example: a man considering matrimony. Suppose I ask him, 'Well, are you going to marry Martha or Mary?' How are we or he to take this? As a question about fact or about choice? Does the distinction still hold or is it mixed up?

Does the 'Will—Shall' uncertainty in English (even when it is shrouded in the mists of 'going to' or of 'I'll') straddle fact and choice?

I shall marry Mary: prophecy?
I will marry Martha: resolution?

compare

I should marry Mary: duty?
I would marry Martha: discretion?

Does this dimmed delicacy of implication register the failure of a pre-Freudian view of motivation to establish itself? (But perhaps, without any of Freud's help, a prediction of future action and a record of present choice have always been hard enough to separate. 'Choices' I call these decisions—these elections to do or to be—perhaps on the Eumenides principle, to placate. They can be unwitting and compulsive enough.)

The trouble with such an example is that it is NOT AN EXAMPLE. An example should be a clear instance which represents a general case. But my *man considering matrimony* may be doing anything you CHOOSE—in your interpretation—to have him be doing. He is an invitation to you to be novelists for the nonce!

(This, incidentally, is one of the main technical obstacles to linguistic philosophy: that its examples—without which it is nearly helpless—are almost never examples. They are challenges to literary resource and sagacity. They are not so much occasions to examine fact as to exercise CHOICES.)

And *this* is my first chief point: to a much greater extent than we profess we communicate through offerings of CHOICES, not through presentations of FACT.

Our statements of fact themselves must be buoyed up, if they are to float at all, on invitations to consent to CHOICES of meaning. The indicative (or assertive) is an abbreviating device for co-ordinating our CHOICES and the optative is the indispensable mood.[1]

---

[1] Some further speculation on this topic will be found in the later chapters of my *Interpretation in Teaching*.

My second chief point is that CHOICES can generate VALUE. It is very frequently the other things a man *didn't* choose to do, the rest of the choice-field, the possibilities he gave up (the girls he did not marry), which put its value charge on the line he took.

The most important choices—and it is these which generate the strongest values—are, evidently, choices as to how we will in future choose. These join the major purposings and they may be organized in an immense variety of ways. The cultures, you may probably agree, could—if we knew enough about them—be described in terms of the organizations they permit and exclude. Within them, these commitments, these self-engagements should, I suggest, be given special prominence in this discussion. And I would recommend the name TROTH for them because of its peculiar relation to TRUTH.[1] This Group's main concern: *Science and Values*, could, I think, be well formulated as:

'The interplay and conflict between Troths and Truths.'

(I would urge that TROTH be pronounced to rime with *oath*, as in *betrothed*; there is affinity between their meanings. The alternative pronunciation somewhat suggests a piggery.)

For Science, the ruling choice (which sets up the criteria for TRUTHS) is the choice to choose thenceforward (within certain wide domains) according to certain rules (principles of choice). Let me call these: Rules of Scientific Conduct.

These get more or less formulated from time to time as the history of investigation calls for one stress or another. That these Rules are not completely and clearly and permanently codified does not diminish their authority. On the contrary, perhaps?

Recalling now some recent discussions of this Group,

[1] For further discussion see my *How To Read a Page*, Index.

you will allow me to take Religion—without attempted definition—as representative of the Values you have been most concerned with. (We must all regret that we must use our words thus loosely; but we are met together for an hour or so, not for life.)

You will have seen that I am about to remind you of or present you with a CHOICE here—made or in the making: How should we choose the TROTHS (choices as to how we will choose) that set up a Religion?

Could they be the same as those which set up Science: to choose by the Rules of Scientific Conduct? I suppose to some they may seem so; to T. H. Huxley replying to Charles Kingsley's letter on the death of his son:

I know what I mean when I say I believe in the law of the inverse squares, and I will not rest my life and my hopes upon weaker convictions.

The rhythm can make us doubtful.

For the majority, however, the Rules of Science and Religion will not be the same, nor will the majority feel that they should be. For most Religions, their adherents are *betrothed* to other principles of choice. Of course, there will be all degrees of fidelity. And these other principles will differ *precisely at their most important points* from the Rules of Scientific Conduct, and in especial as to that part of Scientific Conduct which is the criticism of evidence. Indeed it is the Rules of Religious Evidence which chiefly separate Religion from what is not Religion.

And as they vary they separate the religious from one another—deeply or not as the case may be.

You will be wanting—I hope—to ask this question: In setting up an opposition so between Science and Religion, what do you think you are doing? Is *this* activity Science or Religion, or a mixture, or neither? Is the opposition a *finding* of duly criticized scientific inquiry, or is it something else claiming another sort of authority? Under what

141

Rules (Scientific, Religious, or Other) is this game being played?

It can be embarrassing—very—to realize that this question: 'What are we doing?' MOST needs to be asked about our attempts to answer it. Every attempt to divide or distinguish types of activity NBoughtNB to ask of ITSELF: 'What am I?'

(Would it be unfair to remark that such attempts almost never do?)

This is (or should be) the perennial embarrassment of Philosophy: it must PRETEND it knows how to behave even while seemingly inquiring into how it ought to behave. It must seem to know how to inquire even while inquiring into the very Rules of Inquiry.

This embarrassment (as I have called it) is really the throne: the charge and task—that of inventing (where inventing is both finding and making) a Supreme Ruler in us which can be justified by its ability to unite under itself, BE in itself, the interests which, without such a Ruler, war with one another in shifting alliances for ever.

A wild dream—as wild as a UN (San Francisco model)? What an ill-omened abbreviation *un*, as ill-omened as the name of its early location: 'Lake Success'! A wild dream but an old one—

This plank from the wreck of Paradise, cast on the shores of idolatrous Greece,

to use Coleridge's words about Plato.

Buddhism, Hinduism, Judaism, Platonism, Christianity, Islam, and numberless more local religions have claimed to offer such authority—NOT, I take it, as truth-systems analogous with Science but as hierarchical organizations of CHOICES (and thereby of Values) structured and stabilized—and transmitted from generation to generation—by custom and myth, ritual and creed, and all the intricate accountancies and sanctionings of social status.

Into all these varied patterns of TROTHS now comes Science: a system organizing its choices on quite another principle and very much a rival, a claimant to the supreme throne (not only in the popular, the lay mind). This other principle I take to be the undertaking to make choices 'according to the Rules of Scientific Conduct'.

The observance of this undertaking, it is worth noting, is made much easier for the adept by the grim and relentless *fact* that, if he breaks it, the further work in his field will show him up. And to the first man who finds him out, to show him up will be not only advantageous professionally but a point of duty.

Science does not, however, satisfy the needs which the Religions more or less provided for. That, I imagine, is why some of you are here this evening. It would be interesting to know if any of you have any hopes that in time Science will grow into something which could.

I, for one, do not think it can without considerable changes in ˢʷthe Rules of Scientific Evidenceˢʷ.

One such change might be a change in our working concept of 'experience'. Empiricists, though they may admit, if pressed, that there is more to experience than its sensory (or perceptual) side, commonly narrow it down to sensory perception when they talk of hypotheses, conceptual schemes, propositions . . . being verifiable, corrigible, subject to the control of experience or observation.

But there is the world of wish, desire, love, hate, hope, fear, and so on, which we experience—not through sensory perception but—in another way and as directly.

This is the world whose dramatic texture is choice.

As we deliberate—balance—at the parting of the ways we can ʾknowʾ an immense amount about our leanings. We know it, though, in some other way than through

(*a*) sensory accompaniments,
(*b*) reverberations from them,
(*c*) images,
(*d*) verbal formulations or indications of the alternatives.

(Compare how we know that a word we are *not* using has meanings which may mislead, or overtones which would be unsuitable.)

We may be mistaken, of course, in this other mode of awareness; but so we can in sensory perceiving. Science, however, has developed a very advanced technique of *comparison* for sensory perceptions and incredibly refined procedures for reducing them to and replacing them by *measurements*. It is at home to the measurable. Hence its hospitality to sensory observations; it knows how to entertain them. It does not yet know what to do with all the rest of the information by which we guide our lives.

Science thus is at a loss as to those modes of self-control (of feed-back and feed-forward) our skill in which has given the religions their authority. But that authority is not mere power, such as a magician might be supposed to possess. It is moral mastery; and here renunciation as a source of value may be borne in mind. The difference in our feelings toward great religious founders and toward great men of science belongs to those deliveries of non-sensory knowledge of which I have been speaking. So does the self-knowledge from which these feelings draw their sanction.

But, alas, these remarks suffer from the uncertainty which attached to that wooer of Martha or Mary. We are being invited to become biographers and the very figures we contemplate are projections of our choices. How to read such evidence and how to criticize it, how to allow for or control its fluctuations: these are problems which do not belong to Science as we at present conceive it. And the very virtue which has grown up with Science (rectitude in the presentation of data and procedures), a virtue which may be the most promising new thing in human development, impels us to look with warranted suspicion upon alleged knowledge so dubious in its origins as this. A Gandhi at a crisis can say: 'Ultimately we are guided not so much by the intellect as by the heart' and we can approve that *he* should be so guided; but not every 'heart-grasp' is to be trusted. 'Heart-grasps' indeed can be man's worst bane. Hence the need for criticism. But how are we to develop, *as Science*, a critical regard for these guiding intimations from our innermost selves—without wrecking everything in the attempt? The dangers are familiar.

Science, unless we limit it prematurely and unfairly, does look like the harbinger of man's fulfilment. Do not let us forget how young Science still is. On its own time-scale and in its own picture of how we and our powers have come about, it is hardly more than a strange sport of an experimental embryo as yet. It has had so little experience and already it has such gigantic powers. And they are accelerating beyond our grasp.

The most alarming of its powers to me concern education. Premature attempts to be scientific in education seem to me as likely to devastate promising segments of mankind as any other peril I have heard of. People could so easily be deprived—for their good, it would be thought —of the means of learning how to order their choices.

In the theory and practice of education—the learning of the conduct of the mind—it would be best, for a long time to come, to develop the sciences of control *without applying them*. But I do not see this happening. Otherwise—like old-style archaeologists—we may destroy the very possibilities we hope to profit from. The judgment as to what is or is not an improvement in humanity is not at present within the competence of Science. Yet we have, I think, to seek a way by which Values might unrestrictedly come into the care of Science.

XIV

Poetry as an Instrument of Research[1]

ALL I will do, can do, need do is draw your full attention to these three fine words:

POETRY as an INSTRUMENT of RESEARCH

held together for a while in this non-committal pattern by the small, unobtrusive words: '*as*', '*an*', and '*of*'—words not too small but too recondite and subterranean in their working to be discussed tonight. I think of these busy little particles as bureaucrats, palace officials, powers behind the throne; and of POETRY and RESEARCH, at least, as very much Public Figures, accustomed to the admiring or sceptical scrutiny of crowds and possessed too of a corresponding power of being, if need be, all things to all men.

Suppose now I make a very slight physical change—write *is* for *as*, and pronounce accordingly. Compare:

Poetry as an Instrument of Research

Poetry is an Instrument of Research

This little change in one letter, possibly in one phoneme only, by putting the words into an assertorial clip, can alter everything: their meanings, the behaviour of their meanings to one another, and to their readers, their readers' attitudes to the various resultants they may then make up and to the possibilities of each word as joining in.

[1] Notes for a talk to a group of students of English.

We may easily imagine this inadequately, and suppose that the assertion merely pushes forward, otherwise unchanged, something which was much the same before. Or that it only invites the innumerable cogwheels of logic to engage. But in many cases, and in the most interesting and important cases, those in which thinking—as distinguished from routine manipulation—is most going on, what happens will be much more complex than that. Possible meanings for [sw]Poetry[sw] and for [sw]Instrument[sw] and for [sw]Research[sw] will then have to consult, and negotiate, sacrifice and yield and push, undertake and contract —enter indeed into a joint commitment and prepare at least tentative policies to meet eventualities. All this— and much more—as the immediate outcome of the replacement of an *as* by an *is*.

Minds have often enough been compared to central telephone exchanges. It may be more profitable to compare the formation of a sentence to a commercial merger or even to a military alliance; and when it is big words which there agree to combine their powers—for certain purposes and in view of this and that and the other in the current situation and these and those possibilities—we are very much more likely to underrate than to exaggerate the complexity of the transaction.

All this if we let the *is* clinch or freeze, as it were, the utterance, giving it the solidity, fixity, rigidity of responsible prose, if we make the sentence, in short, mean what it says and be ready to take the consequences.

But, of course, we need not do any of this; we can still use an *is*, use, in fact, almost all the linguistic resources of prose, without incurring any of these liabilities.

I once incurred many frowns through calling such sentences, as they occur in much poetry, *pseudo-statements*,[1] trying to indicate thereby that they are not statements,

---

[1] See *Science and Poetry*, 1926, 1935, ch. vi, 'Poetry and Beliefs'.

though grammatically they seem to state; not statements such as the statements which build up science or any fabric of factual discourse. I soon found that among literary folk I could not have done anything less welcome. The most powerful pundits, prelates of the critical world, joined in denouncing me, for what? For saying, as they alleged, that such sentences are *false* statements, and saying this in a peculiarly mean and underhand way. The more I pointed out that I didn't and couldn't mean that because I meant that—as they occurred in the poetry—they are not statements at all, the more I stressed the attractive parallel, *pseudo-carp*, the more I urged that they might—in other settings, prose settings—*be* true or false, but that in the poem they gained by being neither, the more glumly convinced my critics were that I was calling poetry names. I mention this because I feel there should be something to be learned from it, some specific obstacle to understanding to be charted; and I have not yet discovered what it is.

The point here, however, is that there is an important use of words—very frequent, I suggest, in poetry—which does not freeze its meanings but leaves them fluid,[1] which does not fix an assertorial clip upon them in the way that scientific prose and factual discourse must. It leaves them free to move about and relate themselves in various ways to one another. Probably this freedom should be thought of as a matter of degree, but as degree suggests measurement and we are not in sight of measurement here—do not know what we should seek to measure—we can do no more at present than recognize a necessity of vagueness. That is not to say, however, that the meanings in these fluid sentences are vague. They may or may not be —as meanings in rigid prose may or may not be. *Vagueness-precision* and *rigidity-fluidity*, as I am suggesting we use them here, are different dimensions. In fluid language

[1] See *Interpretation in Teaching*, ch. xxiii.

a great many very precise meanings may be free to dispose themselves in a multiplicity of diverse ways.

This may well be exceptional—be limited to the performances of vigilant readers rather than be a normal outcome of the interrelations of the words. Precision is ordinarily the result of a word's need to relate its meanings to the meanings of other words in the sentence, the paragraph, and so on. The assertorial clip usually heightens precision by forcing words to take better account of one another, though the problems which thereby arise may be solved by resort to indefiniteness.

It is important not to forget the extreme tenuity and precariousness of the grounds of any such remarks as these: one man's actual experience and his imaginings of the experience of others. So much critical writing proceeds in so serene a neglect of this immitigable isolation that we are taken in—as by an inverse conjuring trick— and think that is public which must necessarily be private. But perhaps this oblivion of the circumstances of such communications is a favourable condition for their success.

Let me now use the privilege of a definer and invite you to mean—for this occasion—by ᵗPoetryᵗ (ᵗ. . .ᵗ for technical) words so used that their meanings are free so to dispose themselves: to make up together whatever they can.

You will agree, I think, that we have a grand old tradition against words so used, words whose meanings are free to move about. It dates—does it not?—from Socrates. If the meanings of words are free to move about, then there can be no pinning an opponent down, no convicting him of self-contradiction, no catching him out shifting his ground; indeed none of the rules of that amusing old game will hold. The comedy of argument and its practical purposes alike depend upon a convention of constancy in meaning. In ʳPoetryʳ, as I have just defined it, the poignant humour of the *Euthyphro* would be impossible. It depends—does it not?—on the very contrast between the texture of Socrates' discourse and the bad ʳPoetryʳ Euthyphro has puffed himself up with.

In the preface which the translator has written for the Loeb edition there is a richly ironic sentence: 'Instruction in methods of thinking may perhaps seem needless to modern readers: even they, however, may find it interesting, and in Plato's time it was undoubtedly necessary.' I like to compare this with a bit of verbal behaviour emitted by my friend B. F. Skinner in his final William James Lecture: 'The attempt to teach people how to think', he said, 'seems nowadays to have been abandoned.'

To come back to my three big words. In spite of Socrates I am going to leave them, and invite you too to leave them, free to waltz about with one another as much as they please. I will therefore be talking ʳPoetryʳ (in the technical sense given above), not prose.

My three big words are all Princes with plenty of independent power, though they will take turns, as the occasion changes, at serving one another. I have seated (or the Palace Officials have) the ruling power (for this occasion) in the middle and higher up, with his ministers to the right and left:

INSTRUMENT

Poetry   *Research*

It may seem whimsical to make ˢʷInstrumentˢʷ here the overlord, with ˢʷPoetryˢʷ and ˢʷResearchˢʷ as his servants. The rest of this talk is in justification.

ʷPoetryʷ—the making art, the constituting energy—is a word of august rank, and of much studied resources. I need not do more here than remind you once more that ʳPoetryʳ, as I am using it *here*, is words which are free to mean as they please (which need not be 'as you or as I please').

"Research" on the other hand, many will think, is a word in need of rescue, witness the following:

Dear Dr. R.

For a philosophy course at —— University, I am writing a research paper about your book *General Education in a Free Society*.[1] I need some additional information to complete the paper that only you can give me. Will you please check your basic philosophy at the bottom of this letter and return the form to me in the enclosed envelope?

Idealistic   Pragmatic   Realistic   Naturalistic

But education can provide parodies of everything.

Traditionally Poetry and Research have been antagonists. The *Republic* mentions an old feud between them 'of which the signs are everywhere'. To put two such lively words together and feel their tensions and interactions—in the ghostly schemas of the possible settings they can conjure up—while trying meanwhile to find some way of recording the drama, or at least of indicating the different roles and relations their meanings assume: *this* is Poetry at work as an Instrument of Research. There is no technique for it as yet. None the less it is the phase which most matters in thinking; it is where the originative opportunity opens and the germination of the new idea can occur, though, of course, it is the occasion also for the messes and the muddles, the place of confusion, negligence, and mistake. How often, in an individual life, or in the history of a business or of a nation, of an inquiry, a subject or an art, has the new conception, the new power, the new path, been shut off by what looks later on like an obsessive attachment to a routine pattern of attention, a conventional alliance of procedures, a fixed association of aims? How little, it seems later, would have been needed, how slight a shake-up would have been enough, to have

---

[1] I was startled by this attribution till I perceived that each of the other members of the Harvard Committee on General Education would have received a similar letter.

brought the possibilities—so nearly realized and so strangely dormant—into living co-operation!

It is easier to dilate on such 'Might-have-beens!' and 'Why-nots?' than to develop a general remedy. It is not as a remedy but as part of the search for remedies that I am suggesting the encouragement of a poetic concern with the interactions of words—*not* to produce more poems but to induce a heightened and clarified sort of observation of the poetic process *at work*. But, as I use these words I am reminded that a title I offered to a Social Relations Graduate Colloquium—'Words at Work'—naturally appeared on their Bulletin Board as 'Words that Work'. It is not easy to let up on the pressure we are under to get something (as we hope) *said* in favour of our awareness of the process of *saying*. None the less, may some further consideration of some meanings of the word *Instrument* be of some use?

It is an extraordinarily wide-ranging word. And yet this is not surprising since almost anything may be regarded as an instrument: as a tool, an agency, a means, a stage in a process, a circumstance, something in which or with which or through which or by which some outcome may be forwarded. Instruments might be divided into endless kinds and the modes set up for these dividings (the principles of classification) could be highly various. But further, these modes, these principles themselves would be instruments and so would any procedures we might use for sorting or ordering *them*. Concepts—to use a word of parallel scope—are typical instruments and the sighs over lost opportunities which stirred in my last paragraph but one could have been heaved instead over inappropriate instruments.

I suppose that in almost every field of human endeavour the worst doubts—those that could murder the most sleep —are doubts whether we are going to work in at all the right fashion, whether what we are taking for granted, our way of seeing the problem, the skill we are trying to apply, the aim we hope to achieve—though right maybe for *other* undertakings—whether these are fit and proper for THIS. (Let anyone who lives a variety of lives—and who does not?—recollect if this is not so.) However sure of ourselves and our doings we may be, there is always some moment when the doubt arises. To sketch it broadly, it is a doubt whether distinctions, theories, techniques (ways of seeing and doing things) developed in one field of activity to further its purposes will be found of service in another field.

And if we try to ask: 'How different are the fields?' does not our question touch the purposes which make them up and thence spread to the distinctions, theories, techniques (ways of thinking and trying)?

Language has an annoying way of anticipating our utmost intellectual flights with smooth and effortless puns. All meanings are means, are instruments, and inside [oc]Instrument[oc] it is somewhat more than a pun if we find [oc]Instruction[oc], since it is through instruments that we form problems. If so the super-problem is to find means of making the greatest possible variety of means available: the widest and freest choice of instruments. For instruments enter into the work and shape not only the success attained but also the end pursued. It may be hoped that, with further study, these dependences of the problem upon the instruments through which it is set will become clearer. And then the relation of these instruments to those through which the problem can be replaced would come forward. What has been lacking may have been freedom in the development of the instruments needed for this super-problem.

To sum up the constructive intent of this briefly. Might not that condition (which I have hoped my title may illustrate) in which words, being clear of prose engagement, are still as yet free to experiment with one another as to which meanings they may jointly support, the condition I arbitrarily named ˹Poetry˺, be found useful—if only by *slowing down* our propensity to leap before we look —in finding us fresh Instruments all the way up toward the endless arch-inquiry: What are we and what are we trying to become?

Instruction and *Usefulness* are the two words which seem to have most to say about the work—giving things structure—of this graceful and luminous word. Useful instruction! What poetic and practical words! May I quote you a sentence I found this summer written up—above a door I used, many years ago, to go through daily—by a hand which seemed to have been mine: I had forgotten. It is from William Godwin, that singular anarchist, author of *Political Justice*:

The remainder of my time I determined to devote to the pursuit of such attainments as afforded me the most promise to render me useful.

I wish I could recall doing something else about that beyond (so it appears) writing it up—over the emblem of our transitoriness.

XV

The Places and the Figures[1]

WITH a tradition we incur its wars along with the rest and one measure of our participation may be our readiness to suspect. Even a harmless-looking academic sentence may not be exempt: 'In the renaissance, as in earlier times, educated men amplified a subject by drawing it as a matter of course through the topics of invention.' Of these sixteen are intrinsic: definition, division, genus, species, contraries, contradictories, comparison, similarity, dissimilarity, adjuncts, cause, effect, antecedent, consequent, notation, and conjugates. These supply the *artificial* arguments, 'so called because they are discoverable through the art of topical investigation.' In addition there are the extrinsic, *inartificial* arguments, whose source is testimony. The Lucifer-like fall of this word *artificial* (along with *trivial*) is an indication of a shift in the intent of education since then. We are not so sure, now, that we should amplify subjects rather than contract them, and this not merely because, in contrast to the renaissance, we are short of time rather than of books. There is a hidden polemic behind the decline of these studies and another behind attempts to restore them. The handling of language comes so near us that we may with reason wonder whether such a thing as an impartial view of its aims is possible. It is assumed in Piece II that 'view' and 'aim' cannot be thus separated.

[1] A review article published in *The Kenyon Review*, January, 1949.

The occasion for these doubtings and deliberations is supplied by two books[1] which raise the question, without attempting explicit answer, how far Shakespeare and Milton owed their achievements to their school training.

Mr. Clark's book is a rich and very well documented contribution to the history of education, judicious, instructive, graceful, and well ballasted with humour and caution. Sister Miriam Joseph's work is more ambitious and conjectural. It relies largely on T. W. Baldwin's book, *William Shakspere's Small Latine and Lesse Greeke*, as to what the poet's schooling may have been and is chiefly concerned with establishing—through laborious and systematic collation—a close parallelism or equivalence between logical and rhetorical teaching and the work of the figurists of Shakespeare's time. These figurists, of whom Puttenham is the best known, stretched the notion of a figure as 'a form of speech artfully varied from common usage' (Quintilian) to cover—with changed headings and nomenclature—the points handled by others under Logic and Rhetoric. By reclassifying the figures Sister Miriam Joseph succeeds in compiling 'an eclectic handbook' in which each item is discussed in extracts from the Tudor author who in her judgment handles it best.

This was no light undertaking and the labour and skill it has required should be insisted upon. So should the utility of having a clear and well arranged compendium, in their own words, of what Shakespeare's contemporaries thought most worth while remarking about the art of composition. These observations and distinctions sum up a long tradition now abandoned. They are presented here in a form convenient for our reflection and we have an improved opportunity to consider what they were trying

[1] *John Milton at St. Paul's School* : A study of ancient rhetoric in English renaissance education, by Donald Lemen Clark (Columbia University Press, 1948). *Shakespeare's Use of the Arts of Language*, by Sister Miriam Joseph, C.S.C. (Columbia University Press, 1947).

to do and how this differs from whatever current attempts we may be making toward the same general end—improvement of verbal conduct.

Before venturing into these very difficult considerations, there are some relatively minor matters I would like to touch upon and put aside. Sister Miriam Joseph set herself an additional task—the exemplification from Shakespeare of the whole body of these named and described devices of composition. Here occasionally she gives her thesis a shade too much benefit of the doubt, prepossessing a word with a meaning to suit her purpose in a fashion especially dangerous with Shakespeare. She equates *invention*, for example, over-simply with 'finding matter for speech or writing', though its senses of devising, fabricating, discovering, and originating were all current in Shakespeare's time. 'To the Elizabethan, invention meant finding matter for composition' (p. 92) is an assertion which narrows interpretation unduly. It is a very frequent meaning, without doubt, but neither the only meaning nor the most active meaning in Tarquin's cry, 'O what excuse can my invention make?' or in others among the passages she cites. To suppose that it is flattens them out somewhat comically. And in general, it is not, I think, unfair to say that this preoccupation with rhetorical usages has been an obstacle as often as it has been an aid to her comments, which rarely add to or light up the accepted meanings. This in its way is an outcome. These specimens from Shakespeare, arranged in an order strictly parallel to that of her eclectic textbook, do enable us to ask rather pointedly how far this sort of concern with composition is useful in reading. In the 'eclectic handbook' we are identifying the figures through explanations and examples; returning thence to Shakespeare, we should be able to reverse the process and consider what help our now technicalized interest in the figures gives to each passage.

Here I think Sister Miriam Joseph has allowed herself

to be distracted by a collational or biographical aim instructively typical of recent scholarship. The interesting question is surely NOT whether Shakespeare uses a given figure, but what *that* variation from flat writing does for him and for us just there. Sister Miriam Joseph does indeed demonstrate that all the named devices of the arts of language 'with two or three negligible exceptions' are employed by Shakespeare. It is not so clear that the trick of identifying the figure is an aid to the reader; still less that any *conscious* employment of it was part of Shakespeare's method. This whole study seems in fact still to be in danger of forgetting one of the morals which animate and add its undertone of grave concern to *Love's Labour's Lost*.

On the more specific question, 'How far does Shakespeare's use of the devices of language traditionally described in Rhetoric tell us anything about his schooling?' it behooves us, surely, to be extremely wary. Shakespeare, notoriously, will not abide our question. It looks as if he could have picked up almost any lore from anywhere. He, who illustrates so much, could illustrate 'rhetorical theory in its entire scope', if any man ever could, without any need for formal instruction. 'Rhetorical theory in its entire scope' is after all no more than a somewhat chaotic collection of observations made on the ways of lively, venturesome speech and writing. It would be very strange if the liveliest and most venturesome writer did *not* fully illustrate these observed ways. It is a long and hazardous hop from this to the position that 'He shows a grasp of the theory as presented by the various texts through Quintilian.'[1] There are ambiguities of 'grasp' and 'theory' to watch here. No doubt Shakespeare does frequently show acquaintance with the formal discussion of rhetoric, as with how much else in contemporary studies; but we do not suppose him to have had legal or medical

[1] T. W. Baldwin, *William Shakspere's Small Latine and Lesse Greeke*, II, 378, quoted by Sister Miriam Joseph, p. 12.

training. It is very likely that he would be curious about
the arts of language (in the medieval sense of 'art'), but
in so far as he was an artist in the contrasting modern
sense, it would be over-simple to conclude that his practical skill *need* have owed anything substantial to school
studies.

Behind this problem of biography several more important questions lurk: to mention two, as to the kind of proof
such points may admit and as to the pedagogic relations
between precept and example. Sister Miriam Joseph does
not enter upon their discussion. A modern student of the
Topica ('Dialectic is a process of criticism wherein lies the
path to the principles of all inquiries', 101*b*; 'Moreover, it
is well to expand the argument and insert things that it
does not require at all . . . for in the multitude of the details the whereabouts of the fallacy is obscured', 157*a*)
ought, I think, to be deeply troubled, though to be
tolerant toward Aristotle's treatment of dialectic has been
the tradition. The fundamental and double-edged old
question which that treatment clouds and slights is as
curative today as ever: What sorts of persuasion are there?
and to what ends may we reasonably employ them? This
is a question we all hope to dodge. To be local and specific
in this matter: which sorts of points in literary history are
capable of being established with what sorts of security?
When a highly conjectural 'Maybe so!' is the best we can
hope for in a given case, how much collective toil and
elaboration of detail is justified in its pursuit? Academic
tradition (which may doom itself so) is apt to regard such
queries as no more than graduate growing pains. The
purity of the scholar's quest for knowledge is often supposed to sanction no matter what waste of time and talents,
and in many quarters there is genuine ignorance as to
what else a student of literature could be doing. It is well
to remember that more than a little unemployment for
academics is one of the more persistent of the economists'

prophecies. In a time of high competition for needed endowment not many modern literary inquiries are going to be easy to justify.

Two answers are usually given to such gloomy reflections. One is that the inquiry may be of value—however unprofitable in itself—through things encountered on the way. The bootless journey may be through fine scenery. Here there were many short passages of Shakespeare— but these are otherwise available; much lively, if ramshackle, sixteenth-century prose, not easily come at, and the spectacle of a great and derelict endeavour spanning 2000 years. The other answer is that the inquiry may be of value as suggesting other problems, which may be tackled with better hope of outcome. To me this second answer offers comfort and I would help if I could to prepare some of these other problems, among them the ordering of the intellectual ends. But let me turn first to the pedagogic question of precept and example.

We are at present risking the futures of all those to whom we give any sort of teaching that does not shame us upon practices highly contrary to those which Mr. Baldwin and Sister Miriam Joseph believe that Shakespeare underwent, and Mr. Clark describes so carefully in his account of Milton's schooling. If those practices were wise then it is hardly possible that ours are not extremely unwise, and *vice versa*. These schoolrooms present a grim picture indeed to modern eyes—'heroic' is Mr. Baldwin's word for it, and certainly it was not bloodless, the rod was an ever-present threat. 'If the foregrounds be well and thoroughly beaten in'—it has been endlessly remarked before that too many schoolmasters seem to have taken literally this phrase from the directions for teaching the Lily *Grammar*. The children—absurdly young for such work as we think—rose at five; 'class from six to nine; breakfast; class from nine-fifteen to eleven; dinner; class from one to five; supper. After supper, from six to seven, the pupils recited to their fellows what they had learned during the day.' The materials on which all this time was spent were rules from the Lily *Latin Grammar* to be memorized, and *Sententiae pueriles* or *Catonis disticha moralia* to be construed. Later on, there were English sentences from *Sententiae Ciceronis* to be translated and compared with the original and passages from the Psalms, Proverbs, Ecclesiasticus or Ecclesiastes to be rendered in Latin. Erasmus and Terence and perhaps Plautus would supply the lighter fare. At a certain stage a grounding in Cicero's *Topica* prepared the boys to study the one hundred and thirty-two figures of speech of Susenbrotus. 'The method prescribed unremitting exercise in grammar, rhetoric, and logic. Grammar dominated the lower forms, logic and rhetoric the upper. In all forms the order was first to learn precepts, then to employ them as a tool of analysis in reading, and finally to use them as a guide in composition.'

We had better, I think, clearly face any suggestion that this procedure was *responsible* for the excellence in literature of Shakespeare and Milton. Sister Miriam Joseph does not, I think, anywhere state such a view. The nearest she comes to suggesting it is perhaps in the following (p. 10): after memorizing Ovid, 'A form would recite to the one next above it, which in turn would recite to the one higher.' (I can just hear them.) 'Thus were poetic rhythms, as distinguished from mere metre, fixed in the ears of the students as an aid in writing verse. Elizabethan poetry illustrates the results of this method.'

I hardly know to what place or figure Fraunce or Puttenham would have assigned this use of 'illustrates'. Possibly it is best considered under 'Notation'. In Sister Miriam Joseph's summary (p. 339), 'When a word is regarded as a word, it is called a notation, that is, a mark representing a sound. As such it may shed light on the thing it names through its etymology, or it may occasion ambiguity or obscurity. . . . From the fact that a word or notation may have a number of different meanings arises ambiguity, sometimes inadvertent, sometimes deliberate.' Fraunce, however, like logicians in many ages, prefers to hand a prime problem here to others: 'So in Notation, the interpretation of the name, seemeth rather the dutie of a dictionary, then of any Logicall institution . . . it seemeth also a Rhetoricall agnomination.' 'Agnomination' here is Fraunce's way of saying 'pun', fifty-five years before the first appearance of that handy word. (Incidentally, Fraunce's reference to a dictionary makes better sense today than in terms of any dictionary existing in 1588). It is not clear, however, how far the figures of ambiguity can help us with what 'illustrates' may be doing here. It might be *syllepsis of the sense*—the senses combined being 'to set in a good light' and 'to confer honour on' as well as, perhaps, 'to exemplify'. We may hope the figure is not *schematismus*: 'when the Orator propoundeth his meaning by a circuite of speech, wherein he would have that understoode by a certaine suspicion which he doth not speake' (Peacham's definition). We may be wrong, however, in supposing any figure to be present. Quintilian's definition reads: 'a form of language *artfully varied* from *common usage*.' We may take 'Elizabethan poetry illustrates the results of this method' as an instance of a type of statement which is common usage, routine rather than artful, standard practice rather than a variation. But then Quintilian's definition itself, if we look at it hard, seems very odd. Are there not plenty of things we would wish to call figures which are in conformity with, indeed prescribed by, common usage—from 'My dear Sir' onwards? 'Usage', too, if we will consider it, will appear to be a very shifty word to be given such responsibilities.[1]

---

[1] I have examined this treacherous custom at some length in *Interpretation in Teaching*, ch. xv and xvi, in the hope of persuading the careful

Sentences like 'Elizabethan poetry illustrates the results of such methods' merit and will repay more attention than they commonly get. It would help a lot if they were generally recognized for what they are—necessarily void, inevitably misleading, formally incompetent. They do not have the structure needed to do what they profess to be doing. They assume a view of causality which is altogether over-simple. Educators have been patiently trying for some fifty years—with only slight success so far, it is true—to discover something reliable about the causal connections between teaching procedures and outcomes. This sort of confident blindness to the complexities is among the chief obstacles. In this instance common sense can detect the absurdity; not so in all cases. And I do not think the logical and rhetorical tools presented in this volume are a sufficient supplement to common sense in the undertaking. We must conclude, I believe, that even were it established that Shakespeare had received the most thorough school grounding in the figures through precept and practice, nothing would be proved either as to his debt to it or as to any general desirability of such modes of teaching.

All this, however, leaves many possibilities open. Some sort of systematic study of some at least of the devices of language so painstakingly labelled and arranged by these logicians, rhetoricians, and figurists may still be what education chiefly lacks. We may decide that the treatment reported and summarized by Sister Miriam Joseph is not the right treatment (and for more than a century few teachers have had any doubts upon this) without denying the need for treatment. Behind the proliferations of nomenclature and the upside-down practices of these old-time pedagogues, there was an aim which we have

that it is unwise to found our attempts to guide language on words which themselves so much need control. No wonder the attempts founder (if so limping a specimen of paronomasia may be pardoned).

often lost sight of. They did at least direct their pupils' attention upon the *means* employed in language—if they came short in consideration of ends. By contrast, without much improving our understanding of these ends, we have in our schools almost entirely left out concern for the means. I am exaggerating here. We have, it is true, made a glorious advance in our regard for regularity in spelling. We have done away—in the schools—with our liberty to spell words to suit our pleasure and our purpose. And since the Dictionary assumed Divine Right, our freedom to trim and embellish our words departed with our freedom in spelling. Prosthesis, epenthesis, proparalepsis (or paragoge), not to mention metathesis and antisthecon, have been banished along with aphaeresis, syncope, synaloepha, and apocope[1] as means of rhythming our discourse, varying our orthography (and teasing the printer). We have set up a cult of uniformity here which has sensibly diminished the power of the pen. We have preferred rigidity (with some gain in mechanical convenience) to flexibility and resource and their attendant risks. And this regrettable interference, which has standardized us where we least needed ruling, has barred the natural way toward the improved spelling which English has needed so badly. A sad example this of the dangers of reform on the wrong level.

Probably we should be glad that the influences which were ready to standardize such an inconvenient and senseless spelling did not make any comparable attempt to freeze composition. Grammar suffered a little, as with the legendary rule against the split infinitive, but the itch to regularize did not reach the places and the figures. This whole world of effort—so long a prime focus for the teacher—enjoyed instead an increasing and protective neglect. So much so that when not long ago some of the very same concerns revived which had originally prompted the

[1] See *Shakespeare's Use of the Arts of Language*, pp. 51–4.

Topica and the *Rhetoric*, not many of those who set out, behind 'anti-metaphysical' or 'non-Aristotelian' banners, to teach us all how we should talk, evinced much curiosity about the ancient highways heading into their well-advertised new territory.

Doubtless they were justified. Few things are harder than to use, in the interests of one sort of metaphysics, work fed from and guided by another. Semantics had too much to do in making some observations on a few choice vices of language and contriving some corrective exercises, to bother with ancient remedies which might even seem to exploit and encourage these vices. It is more surprising that our modern theorists in Rhetoric, though they have described types of ambiguity, obliquities, transferences . . . which extend and deepen the catalogued varieties of interactions between meanings, have been nearly as slow to use the work of their forerunners. The dusty state of the materials may in part explain this and Sister Miriam Joseph's book will help here. The antic nomenclature of the figures and our not unfounded distrust of old-fashioned terms in Logic are added grounds. Still more dissuasive perhaps has been the feeling that the old treatment was encumbered with an over-elaborated, elsewhere directed methodology which would distract imaginative insight rather than stir it. In brief, we fear codification in these matters and with good reason.

Against the old treatment a number of charges, of varying gravity, may be brought. The least might be a certain recklessness or frivolity of purpose. It is amusing but not reassuring to notice how often the inducement offered is that this study 'helpeth to amplify any kind of speech and make it more copious', or 'copiously to dilate any matter or sentence.' An automatic aid to long-windedness, we may exclaim, perhaps unfairly. We are not schoolboys short of matter. It is worse when we are told that we will be enabled 'to fortifie and make stronge our assercion or sentence, to prove and defende, by the force and power of art, things passyng the compasse and reach of our capacitie and witte.' These, we may nowadays think, are the very things we should be taught NOT to be assertive or persuasive about. Wittgenstein's 'Whereof we may not speak, thereof we must be silent', despite its equivocation, may well seem to us safer doctrine. From *Gorgias* onwards too much in the literature of rhetoric has been sales-talk selling sales-talk; and for very good reasons we are more interested today in defensives against than in aids to eloquent persuasion. Though often remarked, this fear and its implications have been little studied. It contrasts strongly with the attitude of a Milton, conscious champion among tongue-fighters and pen-wielders. Perhaps the ideal is changing, at long last. The orator-statesman (along with the warrior-king) may be giving place to another model in the educator's eye. Of course, there have always been those who distrusted eloquence (as there have always been pacifists); but recently perhaps the grounds of the distrust may have widened and improved. We may be adding to our conscious weakness an awareness that in this verbal warfare it is not the opponent's views which get demolished so much as other things of more importance to mankind.

But before we pat ourselves on the back for some new sort of honesty and care for truth, it may be well to go nearer to the sources. Here is a renaissance translation of Isocrates' prose hymn to—Rhetoric, shall we call it? But what we understand by ᵂRhetoricᵂ is, of course, just the question:

> To speak effectually of the full force of this science, we shall finde nothing done with reason which hath not been brought about by the helpe of Eloquence, so that she remaineth the chiefest guide of all our thoughts and deed, being the only instrument of the wise and learned.[1]

[1] *Nicocles*, 9, Thomas Forrest's translation, quoted by Clark, p. 9.

Without supposing her to be the peculiar mistress of the ambitious and the facile, we are likely to think that the early definition, 'so to speak as to gain the assent of the audience as far as possible,'[1] ought to be a clear warning. The assent of the audience may have every sort of motives, and our judgment of audiences may incline us to doubt whether success with them is any good evidence of the soundness of what has been said.[2] If so we are back clearly, in the earlier pages of *Gorgias*, siding with Socrates on the important difference between inducements to belief and instruments of instruction.

Perhaps this return to the sources may be our best way to search our own minds on what is still a frontier problem—discussed today most often as the place of emotive components in discourse. Isocrates, as defender of Gorgias, may help us to remember that the conduct of this search of the mind is itself the prize for which the opposing forces endlessly struggle and intrigue. What I have just quoted from him is a renaissance interpretation. A modern translation reads:

If we sum up the character of this power, we shall find that no reasonable thing is done anywhere in the world without logos, that logos is the leader of all actions and thoughts, and that those who make most use of it are the wisest of mankind.[3]

There seems to be a world of difference between these versions. 'What is speaking here for what?' seeks precedence over the apparently more manageable question: 'What is being said?' Isocrates was at nearly if not quite as much pains as Plato himself to claim superior integrity, a more perfect inner order, as the source and aim of the

[1] *Ad Herennium*, I, 2.

[2] It is interesting to recall the connection between the new rhetoric and the Panhellenic ideal. To Isocrates, father of humanistic culture, 'the new dream of national achievement appeared to be a mighty inspiration' (Werner Jaeger, *Paideia*, Vol. III, p. 53).

[3] *Paideia*, Vol. III, p. 89.

education he offered. To him the Socratics were dispu-
tants and their dialectic (eristic, he prefers to call it) little
better than a training in trickery, a corruption of lively-
witted youth. As to what Plato might have thought of the
passage I have quoted, we may remember that at the end
of *Phaedrus* he makes Socrates say of Isocrates: 'Nature,
my friend, has implanted a love of wisdom in the mind
of the man.' A noble compliment to pay a great, lifelong
opponent, the head of your rival school!

The masters perhaps could have understood one another enough to come to some accord. It was another
matter with their followers—especially when one of these
was of the stature of Aristotle. It is arguable that both
rhetoric—as 'that which enabled us to perfect almost
everything we have achieved in the way of civilization'—
and dialectic—as the audit of meaning—fell away within
their authors' lifetimes, that the first became a study of
suasive tricks separable from the criticism of the springs
of the suasion, and the other an intellectual pingpong
unconcerned with understanding. But such an argument
would perhaps exemplify both degenerations. What matters, in any case, is that modern attempts to improve the
conduct of language should recognize how deep the
undertaking must go. It is not enough to be 'non-
Aristotelian' while employing the least acceptable tricks
of Aristotelian rhetoric, or to pursue propaganda-analysis
propagandistically. Nor will it do to disparage renaissance
rhetoric without deeper examination of its aims and
nature than Puttenham, for example, gave them, or indeed
without as deep a self-search into the grounds for the disparagement as a critic can compass. Doubtless the
supreme balance, *phronesis*, and justice which any inquiry
into language theory, language teaching, language control demand, are far away. Still this demand, which any
interest in these matters must, however shyly and remotely,
posit, does—whether we like it or not—rule all our

efforts, if only as the latest, most encompassing, and synoptic principles of the physicist rule his. The strange thing is that of late his principles grow ever wider and deeper, whereas ours . . .

Perhaps I have only been echoing, darkly and yearningly, Richard Sherry in the 'Epystle' to his *A Treatise of Schemes and Tropes* (1550): 'The common scholemasters be wont in reading to saye unto their scholers: *Hic est figura*: and sometime to axe them, *Per quam figuram?* But what profit is herein if they go no further?'[1]

My doubt, though, is whether there ever has been any 'further' in these directions and by these ways. Not because no more of the same sort can be done. It would be possible to double the two hundred or so Tudor figures by magnifying distinctions, but the upshot would be the same. As with other ancillary studies—grammar, prosody, phonetics among them—what was intended to be a help became a hindrance, preventing the student from remembering the true subject of all his study. Rhetoric and Dialectic, quarrelling with one another, jointly forgot their common aim. And now it is not easy to see in these products of scholastic drudgery the issue of an original concern with the salvation of man.

[1] Quoted by Clark, p. 168. What do we gain by being able to name an instance of aposiopesis?

XVI

Dependence of Thought on its Milieu[1]

THIS is not going to be a satisfactory treatment of
the great theme. It is going to play the characteristic, traditional, philosophical trick upon us. It is going
to limit itself by taking up some of the questions which
would have to be considered first—it seems—before any
'satisfactory' treatment could be possible. But these prior
considerations—we may find—themselves preclude 'satisfactory' treatment.

Take a hard look now at my title.

If thought *is* dependent (no doubt in various ways) on
its milieu, then How? and How far? become almost un-
bearably important questions—and not only for historians,
though, perhaps, especially for historians.

The historian is thinking in a milieu, basing his thought
on records and signs of other thinking—other thinking
taking place in other milieus. (It is annoying that the
plural of this word is so unhandy—a word whose chief
utility is in the plural!) To whatever extent thought is
milieu-dependent, then—centrally for him, less centrally
for those other thinkers—the familiar, ever-present, ever-
unanswered question rises: 'Just what is this dependence
doing to my stuff and what will it do to it when it is taken
(as it will be, if there is to be any point in it) into yet other
milieus?'

[1] A talk given to the Harvard Graduate History Club, in 1951.

It may seem at times—that is, in certain milieus—something more than a smart crack to say that histories are good sources for the periods they are written *in*, to the extent that they distort what they are written about.

But—and here I must ask you to consider anew my title—even already we may each of us have been thinking about widely different things.

'Dependence', what's that? An inescapable control, or the loose sort of influence that an audience may have upon a speaker?

'Thought', what's that? Direction of attention ('I am thinking of *x*, not *y*') or the logical or other concatenation of ideas?

'Milieu' above all, what's that? Philip drunk—Philip sober, or the entire menagerie including the *zeitgeist*?

And, as to INDEPENDENCE, is that the superiority to circumstance of Plato's ideal hero or the insulation of the idiot?

And how far, as each one of us mulls over such choices in his own reflection, how far is what he thinks of and what he thinks of it, itself being guided for him by this perhaps illimitable variety of possible participations we can so lightly refer to as the milieu?

The general theme has, you see, the philosophic earmark: it requires us to understand it fairly deeply before we can begin inquiry.

However, let us begin.
Here is a contemporary biological view:

In general every trait and tissue of the organism develops under the joint influence of the whole constellation of genes and of the environment.[1]

[1] Dobzhansky, *Scientific American*, September 1951, p. 55.

And equally, of course, the functioning of every element thus developed is subject to their interdependencies and to whatever they may be sensitive to—as thus related.

This, to some, is the thought of all thoughts they least enjoy lingering with. It seems to them to destroy individuality, originality, spontaneity—indeed to destroy their very selves. I would suggest that it does NOT, though it may considerably change them: change, that is, our conceptions of these things: the meanings we use with these words.

How often has somebody felt, indeed been clear and certain, that something or other would destroy or had already destroyed . . . Christianity, let us say. How familiar in such cases you historians are with the way the threatened thing changes, and with the problem of what —other than the name—has endured. So may it be here with originality, individuality, spontaneity, and the self. By realizing that we are more representative and responsive than we supposed we may become not less but more originative and spontaneous as individuals and thereby more responsible than we thought.

Let us think now, for a brief while, about what it is in one man or another which may be more or less all these. We call it in the broadest and most generic fashion: THOUGHT. What may we usefully distinguish within this activity which seems so radically to be us?

Consider this diagram . . . (Here consult, if needed, pages 26 to 38.)

The diagram, you will recognize as you puzzle through it, is far more a way of raising questions than of answering any. But it can alter the probabilities as to which questions will arise. And that is, from the point of view of 6, its Purposing, 7.

Purposing, if you ask for a theory about it (1 and 2)

can hardly be made more than a puzzle. It is too central. That is why I have put it at the hub of my wheel. But it can be observed in others, is indeed, for good biological reasons, the most observable macroscopic feature of behaviour. Consider how early the infant becomes responsive to its mother's intentions. It is her Purposing—via 6—which organizes the countless minutiae of her behaviour into recognizable patterns, into a smile or frown, for example. And it is Purposing which builds and unbuilds the most modifiable parts of behaviour. Accordingly we will do well to keep the centrality of Purposing in view as we turn to consider what the milieu may do to these activities which we call our Thought.

Let us try picturing the milieu first as a set of concentric spheres with the thinker at the centre. To discuss these spheres, their relations to one another and to the thinker, would be to discuss all the problems there are.

Obviously, we can't do that here; but—it is worth noting—no one ever—even in the longest volume of Gifford Lectures, nor any group even with all the scope of an encyclopaedia at their disposal—can do more than *sketch* how these things may seem. I stress this because it is most important not to let ourselves be daunted by our own or other people's sketches in this matter. If I may, for the moment, shrink the illimitable *ambiance* down by remembering that you are the Harvard Graduate History Club, you will see feelingly what I mean. A Graduate School is a place where people are very likely to be made both near-sighted and cowardly—or, in politer terms, modest and prudent. They are surrounded by people who as to the world of the *examinable* know far more—having had the time and the need to learn it—than they do. But "examinable" here means only: that in which examinations may be held. We cannot too often remember that the world of the examinable in this sense and the world we should be reflecting upon in our most entire and active

moments are not at all the same. I know that there is another side to all this—the justification of a Graduate
School—but you know it too and I need not waste your
time with remarks about that.

To expand again to those vaster spheres upon which
we are dependent.

The vastest, the inclusive, the ultimately controlling,
let us call, here, the Universe. And let us separate it *very
consciously*, very distinctly, and very diligently from any
pictures we may suppose we, or any other men, can form
of it: especially from the pictures astronomers form of the
cosmos. 'It is the business of science to be wrong', I have
heard Robert Oppenheimer remark—with refreshing
candour. How otherwise could it advance? And let us
separate equally this that I am calling the Universe from
any accounts theologians may seem to give. These
accounts are pictures. Pictures are most important—we
shall consider why and how in a few moments. But this
that they may seem to picture is something else: *neti*,
neti, 'not that, not that', as the Upanisads say. About it
nothing can be said, of it no picture can be formed. Anything we may seem to say, any picture we may seem to
form, is not about it but about some account or picture
purporting to be, or mistaken for, it. We, along with all
that we can think of, live within an indescribable.

Nevertheless, men's pictures for that—which perhaps
always contain some picture of man and his relation to that
—are, as you historians well know, among the chief
guides and shapers of his endeavours. They are his aids—
all but indispensable aids—toward finding his place within
this inconceivable.

Perhaps this paragraph from Gilbert Murray's *Five
Stages of Greek Religion* will help here. It is about the attitude of the later Stoics to the Olympian deities:

They are not gods in whom any one believes as a hard fact. Does
this condemn them? Or is it just the other way? . . . You know that

all your creeds and definitions are merely metaphors, attempts to use human language for a purpose for which it was never made. Your concepts are, by the nature of things, inadequate; the truth is not in you but beyond you, a thing not conquered but still to be pursued. Something like this, I take it, was the character of the Olympian Religion in the higher minds of later Greece. Its gods could awaken man's worship and strengthen his higher aspirations; but at heart they knew themselves to be only metaphors. As the most beautiful image carved by man was not the god, but only a symbol, to help towards conceiving the god; so the god himself, when conceived, was not the reality but only a symbol towards conceiving the reality.[1]

Within this sphere of ultimate reserve, let us now try putting a sphere we will call ᵗPhysicsᵗ. We will not equate it to the Physics of any date and we will recognize that it is likely to be—for a long while still, at least—open to vast theoretical transformations. I take it the contemporary physics (allowing for lag) has been—in modern Western history—an immensely influential factor of the milieu. I somewhat doubt that it will go on being so, as thinkers become sophisticated enough to expect further changes. However, the general popular picture of the mathematical forest—the explanatory proposals competing for the sunshine of experimental support—may long continue. It fits in with man's sporting and gambling impulses. Furthermore, Complementarity theorems (see p. 114), metaphorically extended, are likely to have a future. As historians, you will ask yourselves whether, e.g., views formed within different nationality complexes are not thereby put into complementarity relations with one another.

It may now seem natural to put inside ᵗPhysicsᵗ a sphere we might call Culture. Culture here is the kind of thing Anthropology tries to describe. It includes in a very important place those pictures of the Universe and Man I have been talking about. But somewhat significantly, no culture I have heard of will fit *inside* Physics (1950). They

[1] From Gilbert Murray, *Five Stages of Greek Religion*, p. 76.

all ask for liberties and miracles which Physics must deny them. Obviously *spheres* was the wrong word. *Oblate spheroids* would have done better, if you had happened to know what they are: egg-like volumes. My 'concentric spheres' were but an expositor's device and the point is that they are NOT concentric. Our poor thinker, as he lets himself be generated by one or other of them in turn, is dragged hither and thither, and if he is at all obstinate about the consistency of his positions, is in danger of being torn apart. We are all, increasingly perhaps, split personalities: different people in different milieus; for consistency is a principle whose cost of upkeep is exceedingly high. It calls for ceaseless expense of energy and constant sacrifice. Not only (see pp. 30–1) is any one view itself a 'continuously effort-consuming activity' like the maintenance of a state in peacetime, but the resolution of a deep conflict can be as ruinous as a war effort. It is not only nations, alas, that can squander their future in heroism. We all know fanatics who have nothing left over.

Partly because of these high costs and for economy of effort generally (here is an important sub-department of the work of 6) we form habits, routines, constancies and fixities of feeling and conception. These, evidently, are all-important mechanisms (but they are more vital than this word suggests) in the working of the milieu on the mind. The most extensive changes in milieu take no effect if we remain insensitive to them. Habits of thought and feeling are man's great insulators and defences, as psychiatry too well can teach us. The art of thought, the subtlety of genius, is in finding a dimension along which the protectiveness of habits can lapse, and the thinker become open and responsive and subject to forces in the milieu which could otherwise take no hold. Compared with others he then appears to be as free, individual, spontaneous as he is original.

Habits are representatives of past milieus and are at bottom economic and conservative devices; they do not want to be disturbed. Together with them may we group certain faiths and loyalties and resolutions and commitments and convictions: defences likewise against strains that certain aspects of the milieu would impose did we allow them? May I call these the Protective Troths? (See 'Language and Value'.) There could be bitter controversy here, which I will barely escape by asking you to choose your own examples. These decisions—once for all, for good and for ever—as to how we will henceforward decide, deserve our reverence even when we think them disastrously mistaken. They have generated many of the bloodiest stories you historians have had to relate. But, on the other hand, they *have* provided foundations upon which, at times, it has been possible to build. Is building possible without them?

The most sustained, elaborate, intricate, interdependent structure yet raised—the sketchbook of Science—has *that* any such Protective Troths guarding its base? Does Science rest on a faith in at all the sense in which we suppose the religions do? I doubt it. For one thing, I doubt whether this building metaphor fits Science as it has traditionally been thought to fit some of the great religions. They have their foundation creeds; as intellectual structures they parallel their Cathedrals and Mosques and Temples, as they parallel the ecclesiastical, administrative structures they have aspired to. But there is no creed and no administrative headquarters, no court of last appeal, no focus of authority, for Science. In this it resembles its own current picture of the cosmos much more than any edifice. No doubt (see 'Language and Value') there are certain Rules of Scientific Behaviour which the scientist is committed to observe. But these are, I would hold, unwritten, and subject, if need arise, to considerable modification. In any case they are more like the Rules of a Club than the articles and dogmas of the more exclusive religions profess themselves to be.

I have lingered with this last because it is widely felt that the Scientific picture is from now on an even more important part of the milieu than a thinker's class-status, his nationalism, or his religion. And there are those who maintain that attachment to this picture (in one or other of its editions) has become a religion, undercutting, wherever it spreads, the other religions.

The Troths I have mentioned may have seemed negatives: resolves—NOT. But Troths are the most creative events in which man participates. In the writing of a poem, the painting of a picture, there is a Troth positive and prophetic, a Troth with what the work must be. So too in the living of the saint. Moreover it is in such positive Troths that the general trend of the universe seems to be most clearly reversed and higher orders of form emerge. To say this is to use contemporary scientific mythology. It is safer to say that in our Troths we recover—it ineradicably seems so—our control over the milieu and ourselves. We may be, to whatever degree, subject to the illimitable influences I have been so crudely sketching: physically, biologically, socially, psychologically, psychotically in a condition of miserable dependence; but in the quite indescribable passage we call a resolution—indescribable as that inclusive sphere was indescribable and for the same unformulatable reason—this centre which is 'I' can overcome all this, become most respondent to what it has chosen to be most respondent to, and thus discover, in humility or in despair, that what it is most deeply dependent upon is, in some way, itself.

Section Three

XVII

Fifteen Lines from Landor

Suppose that a gale is sweeping over a forest, the trees respond with their varied notes according to all the possible differences in their cavities. What need would there be to pass a judgment on their multitudinous notes or declare that some and not others are the voice of the gale?

Chuang Tzu

'POETRY gives most pleasure', said Coleridge, 'when only generally and not perfectly understood. . . . From this cause it is that what I call metaphysical poetry gives me so much delight.' (*Anima Poetae*, p. 5) The remark, like so many of S.T.C.'s other jottings, deserves more attention and development than it has received.[1] To treat it adequately would require a complete theory of the kinds of understanding and the world is not yet ripe for that. But some immediate advance can be made by a close study of the actual processes of understanding poetry. I shall first describe a method for this study, then present some of its results, and then speculate upon the inferences that may be drawn from these as regards Coleridge's *dictum*, our reading habits, and criticism in general.

[1] The qualification published by Miss Kathleen Coburn (*Inquiring Spirit*, p. 55): 'When no criticism is pretended to, and the Mind in its simplicity gives itself up to a Poem as to a work of nature, Poetry gives . . .' should be borne in mind, but hardly lessens the subversive force of the remark.

We can take any passage of poetry for which 'perfect understanding' is not likely to be too frequent and invite a number of readers (about whom we should, ideally, know as much as we can) to give, in any fashion they please, an account of what they understand by it. In practice, we have to ask for a paraphrase and exposition, leaving it to them to decide which parts require exposition. It is best for this purpose to eliminate, so far as possible, the question 'Is the passage good or bad poetry?' and to invite answers only to the question 'What does it mean?' (or, 'What is it, as a system of meanings?'); which is a different question from 'What does it say?'

These accounts, if the writers have been at all successful, are sets of signs from which we then have to conjecture their various readings of the passage. Here is where the difficulties and dangers of the method occur. What we take as their readings of the passage are only our interpretations of accounts which will as a rule be very inadequate and sometimes very misleading. However, in a large number of accounts of the same passage, we shall usually discover instructive groupings and very different accounts often throw helpful light on one another. Through this rather hazardous work of interpretation we arrive at a representative collection of readings. These, in the ideal case—in which all our own interpretations were correct and the accounts themselves sufficient— would be a collection of specimens of high significance for biology. They would show the history of a set of interpretations, the points at which variation occurs, and the types of variation—the stages in the growth and the occasions for mishap of the most important human function. But ours is not the ideal case, we must be content to use our readings more tentatively and concern ourselves with simpler, which here means less analysed, problems.

A passage which has provided interestingly varied readings is the following (Landor, *Gebir*, III, 4–18):

Tho' panting in the play-hour of my youth
I drank of Avon too, a dangerous draught,
That rous'd within the feverish thirst of song,
Yet never may I trespass o'er the stream
Of jealous Acheron, nor alive descend
The silent and unsearchable abodes
Of Erebus and Night, nor unchastised
Lead up long-absent heroes into day.
When on the pausing theatre of earth
Eve's shadowy curtain falls, can any man
Bring back the far off intercepted hills,
Grasp the round rock-built turret, or arrest
The glittering spires that pierce the brow of Heav'n?
Rather can any with outstripping voice
The parting Sun's gigantic strides recall?

The readers who supplied the accounts of its meaning
that I am about to use were men and women studying
English Literature at Cambridge or Harvard and Rad-
cliffe. The authorship of the passage was not told them,
and no one guessed it.

*May I strongly recommend those who wish to gain all the
insight that the following specimen interpretations can afford,
to take paper and pencil and write out their own paraphrase
before reading further. Without intimate familiarity with
the specific problem the adventures of other readers lose their
instructive power.*

For convenience, we may break the passage into three
sections, lines 1–3, 4–8, 9–15, though a more complete
study would, of course, trace connections between individuals' peculiarities of interpretation in all three sections.
Each section is evidently susceptible of more varied interpretations when taken by itself than when taken with the
rest of the passage, and a first difference between good and
bad readers can be stated simply in terms of the number
of relevant items that they can bring and hold together as

co-operating signs. These items, in such a passage as this, will be of several sorts:

1. The plain literal senses of the words and sentences.

2. The metaphoric senses. These, in most cases, are multiple; within the range of transference from the literal sense (supposing there to be only one) are a number of other senses with various relations to it. Which of these relations serves as the ground of the metaphor, and thus which of the possible metaphoric senses is taken, depends upon what is happening at many other points in the interpretative process. More than one metaphoric sense (and more than one literal sense) *may* be taken by a reader simultaneously, and may need to be taken, as Mr. Empson has, perhaps overwhelmingly, demonstrated.

3. Feeling. Attitudes of the poet to his sense (literal or metaphoric). We may call these *emotive overtones*, if we are careful not to overlook the fact that they are not less important than sense in guiding interpretation.

4. Tone, the poet's manner of address to his reader.

5. Signs of his own critical attitude to his work, of his confidence or diffidence about the success of his intricate endeavour.

6. Signs of his intention which may be larger than can be implemented by the items so far enumerated. For example, omissions, or a choice of form, or of highly developed metaphor in preference to plain sense, may come under this heading.[1]

It is noteworthy that feeling, e.g., will often prescribe words for the sake of metaphoric senses that are superfluous to the main sense-articulation of the passage, but which control feeling. The connections and transactions between these items may be, and frequently are, *inexplicit*, made without any conscious recognition of them by the reader (or by the poet).

[1] For further discussions of these items and their possible inter-relationships, see *Practical Criticism*, Appendix A.

Almost word by word the process of interpretation can be seen—from our accounts—to bifurcate according to the sets of items, of all these sorts, that are taken together.

SECTION ONE

Tho' panting in the play-hour of my youth

1·1   In an idle hour of my youth being restless for something to do.
1·11 Although as a boy in brief pauses of my play.
1·12 When, in my youth, I needed spiritual refreshment.
1·13 Searching in my youth for aesthetic comfort.
1·2   Although at the time in my youth when I frequented plays.
1·21 I too was enthralled by dramatic poetry—as enthralled as a child at the theatre.
1·3   When eager and careless, in the irresponsibility of youth.

I drank of Avon too, a dangerous draught,
That rous'd within a feverish thirst of song,

1·4   I (like Shakespeare) drank of the river Avon.
1·41 'Avon too' may mean 'Avon as well as other poets', or 'I have done what other people have done', or 'of the same rich draughts that Shakespeare drank'. The third is the least likely, the first the most.
1·42 He became inspired to write poetry, by drinking of the river Avon, our local Helicon, which had inspired Shakespeare.
1·43 Although I read Shakespeare also (as well as doing other things).
1·44 By 'thirst of song' is meant 'thirst of singing'.
1·45 There is something definitely comic in the thought of over-indulgence in the reading of Shakespeare as an act of youthful heedlessness.
1·5   I drank in the spirit of the countryside.
1·51 The beauty of the river Avon aroused in me the desire for self-expression.
1·6   Although overcome by passions in my youth, I thought deeply and thinking maddened me.
1·61 In the days of his youth when life was still a game, tho' a hard one, the writer turned to Shakespeare to refresh his spirits, a questionable resort because the study of poetry is as likely to be discouraging as refreshing. . . .

Hitherto I have not commented upon these specimens of interpretation. I am not here concerned to defend or arraign them as products of our educational system. They are facts of natural science to be inquired into as best we may. The last example is sufficiently curious to be quoted in entirety. It continues:

> He hopes that his soul may never be so discouraged as to experience the deep pangs of torture of which it is capable and which, once started, are never quite soothed away. That while yet able to enjoy life he may not find his convictions shattered, his mind groping in Despair for Truth where all is confusion and where Truth cannot be found. That he may not revive from the past stories of tragic heroes to bring dismay into the hearts of others.

Whether such a reader is likely to benefit from a university, or how he came there, are questions for another occasion. Here the medical interest of studies of interpretation is more to the purpose. Such an extreme case brings out clearly something which is very frequently apparent in accounts given of the meaning of almost any passage—that personal preoccupations are strong enough to override everything and twist any pointers into directions governed by the reader's own volitional situation. We shall see further examples, in what follows, of these extraneous interventions, factors of interpretation which prevent communication from occurring. Their theoretical importance is that they show how, in normal communication, similar volitional factors (but not irrelevant ones) are at work.

SECTION TWO

Yet never may I trespass o'er the stream
Of jealous Acheron, nor alive descend
The silent and unsearchable abodes
Of Erebus and Night, nor unchastised
Lead up long-absent heroes into day.

The duplicity of *may* ('I cannot', 'I hope I shall not') acted as a main pivot, but both what the poet could not

do and what he would not do varied widely and for
equally diverse reasons:

CANNOT

2·11   He cannot go into the past, into the place of death, nor search
out again the heroes—poets—that have died.

2·12   True intimacy with the spirit of such a past hero (as Shakespeare) is naturally denied us.

2·121 He feels that he can never do more than catch glimpses of
this beauty, that he can never know the man through his
works. . . . The last two lines (13–15) obviously refer to
Shakespeare alone.

2·13   I concluded that I could never write of the other world (as
Dante), nor treat, without much criticism, of old epic
heroes.

2·131 Now I realize that I can never recover in their fulness the
exploits and characters of the heroes of poetry just as I cannot look upon the dead.

2·14   I shall never be able to write any poetry myself.

2·15   But I shall never live to solve the secrets which those dead
heroes knew. (Cf. comment on 1·61?)

2·151 But never will I be able to make convincing and immortal
the phenomena of life, the hidden secrets of the universe.
(Cf. comment on 1·61).

2·152 I cannot pierce beyond Death, or in life discover its secrets;
nor can I, with impunity (an unnecessary phrase: he couldn't
do it at all), call up again the heroes of the past.

2·16   Yet even Shakespeare I found difficult enough. How much
the less then may I attempt to fathom the writings of the
Ancients whose works must ever remain a closed book to
me.

2·17   Yet I shall never arrive at this so desirable and far-off land.

2·18   All the poem seems to mean as a whole is that the gentleman
liked poetry and wished he could shake the hand of Shakespeare and perhaps get his autograph.

2·19   But I should not be able—even if I had the cheek to try
—to accompany Homer, Virgil or Dante to Hell. That sort
of thing is over now.

WOULD NOT

2·21   Yet I should never want to go down to Hades alive.

2·211 I have never wanted to learn to play music which would help me, like Orpheus, to cross Acheron and bring back dead heroes from Hell.

2·22   Yet may I never descend in my lifetime to the practice of dragging to light the deeds, perhaps unworthy, of heroes long dead.

2·02   He tried to write of dead heroes and evil-doers.

2·221 Yet may I never try to do impossible things.

2·23   Not that I wish to invent impossible stories of my adventures in Hades.

2·24   He hopes that he will never, in choosing subjects for his writing, go back to classical material or any material characicistic of another age.

2·241 Yet may I never write of Greek mythology, for to do this sort of thing properly one must live in the times when Greek mythology was believed in.

2·242 I did not want to write of past deeds and classical lore, because I found that I could not handle such subjects worthily.

2·25   I hope I may never, like epic writers, lose touch with life, to trespass over Acheron which would be jealous of my enjoyment of mundane pleasures.

2·251 I realise that the epic writer, the man who merges an exact philosophy of life with the study and enjoyment of living things, has failed to perceive that man cannot go beyond expediency. (Cf. 1·61?)

2·26   The rest of the poem, after the first three lines, expresses the idea of the vanished sunlight of youth. It is a wistful retrospection toward a youth now worn out. In contrast with youth is the darkness of the underworld, an underworld from which the speaker is unable to draw back the friends of his youth. He can draw them back, but he is *chastised*. He then is pained by his past excesses.

2·261 Yet having crossed over into this realm of age and dark, I can never re-emerge with my youth into the day of joy.

The 'regret for vanished youth' and the 'occultism' (2·15, 2·151) prepossessions are, as we shall see, very persistent.

My documentation is becoming somewhat extensive, but I am omitting numerous varieties, several species, and even some genera. It must be remembered that any of these readers might discuss at length Landor's merits or defects as a poet, and even the qualities of this passage —in the pages of *The Criterion*, for example—without ever discovering the discrepancies of their readings. Landor, after all, is not thought to be an unusually cryptic poet. It is a stimulating exercise to attempt to imagine a similar display of readings of one of the Editor's poems, or of Mr. Yeats' *Byzantium*. Among other things it might stimulate the desire to pursue the theory of interpretation further.

SECTION THREE

> *When on the pausing theatre of earth*
> *Eve's shadowy curtain falls, can any man*
> *Bring back the far off intercepted hills,*
> *Grasp the round rock-built turret, or arrest*
> *The glittering spires that pierce the brow of Heav'n?*
> *Rather can any with outstripping voice*
> *The parting Sun's gigantic strides recall?*

Great difficulty was clearly felt (except by those who had read Sections One and Two with unusual sagacity) in bringing Section Three into living connection with them. And odd interpretations of the earlier sections led to attempts to force parallel strangenesses into Section Three. I shall cite only a few special cases.

But even those who left the last section quite unconnected with the rest indulged at times in equally remarkable conjectures:

3·1   When, in an interval of life on earth, a woman's shadow falls like a curtain on a stage, can any man do anything?

The Freudian possibilities in the interpretation of the remaining lines, after this auspicious start, escaped, however, this reader.

The apparent variation in the visual images (it may be only in the phrasing) evoked by 'Eve's shadowy curtain' raises an interesting point of critical detail.

3·2   By night's dark curtains.
3·21   Like a black curtain.

A reader who is unaware of discrepancy of effect here will receive little from poetry. And apart from all accidents of imagery the senses of *black* and *shadowy* support totally distinct feelings.

Attempts to connect 'pausing theatre' with 'play-hour' in part explain some of the following:

3·3   When one's life is drawing to a close.
3·31   At the end of the world's play.
3·32   When the darkness of death falls on humanity.

A pause, however, usually implies a continuation.
Allegories of several kinds were drawn out:

3·33   When the curtain of age falls upon his life, can any man bring back the far-off hills that were his goal, hold fast to the turret of youthful certainties, or stay the disappearing spires of great ambitions. Rather can any man recall his glorious but setting youth?

3·331   When one has reached the end of life, after experiencing its manifestations can he bring back the spontaneity, the convictions, the ambitions of his youth?

3·332   The last seven lines seem to ask whether, as age comes on, any man is able to recapture the poignant visions of youth and express them in song. The mood appears similar to that of Wordsworth's *Intimations*, the light of common day into which the Wordsworth vision fades being here represented by the fall of evening.

3·333   'Intercepted hills'—I think this means the dreams of youth.

3·34   The meaning here resolves itself into a doubt whether *any* man, tho' he be a Shakespeare, can remember the things of life, symbolized by hill, turret, spires, and sun, after he has died.

3·341   If in these lines the writer is alluding to man's exile from Eden, barring him from Paradise, one would have no quarrel with the poet. Perhaps his meaning is that by his own sins he is rendered incapable.

3·35   Can any man when death has taken it from the world, revive and keep alive past greatness?

3·4   Although the huge landscape seems to be standing still as I write—what with Christianity and one thing and another——you cannot do that sort of thing now any more than bring the landscape back this side of the dusk, or stop the Pagan sun from setting (continuation from 2·19).

3·41   How in this twilight of the ages can man bring back and picture vividly the far-off times—the old stories of Mount Olympus as the abode of the gods, or of the rock-built turrets of Greece or Rome, or of the glittering Cathedrals of the middle-ages? The underlying plea is for poetry to turn from the far-off past towards the present.

3·42　No man can fully recapture the spirit of a byegone age.

Most preferred much more literal readings, but not necessarily safer ones:

3·5　As fruitless as for a man to contrive the approach of the horizon or other inaccessible and architectural phenomena.

3·51　Can any one cause the circular turret to leave its rock and approach.

3·52　Stop the glittering spires from piercing Heaven.

3·521　Tried to write of long-dead evil doers, but found it as impossible as it is to grasp the smooth surface of a stone turret or prevent a spire from reaching heavenward.

3·522　Crush the glittering spires?

3·523　Extinguish the stars in the sky?

3·524　Prevent the glistering stars that threaten the brow of heaven?

Some of these last, since they occur after twelve lines of hard reading, may perhaps be set down as effects of fatigue. A majority of readers were content to take the last seven lines as a decorated platitude of the flattest kind.

It is difficult, in giving such a display of interpretation, to avoid the impression that a mere teaching scandal is being exploited, that the utterances of pre-eminent dolts are being elicited and put forward with undue prominence, in brief, that I have been collecting 'howlers'. I have, however, not yet met anyone who thought so whose own critical endeavours would not have added lustre to that aspect of any collection. But it may be useful—to correct this impression that the writers of these paraphrases are not normal readers—to consider briefly a few equivalent examples of interpretations by more mature students. They will help us to remember that the most eminent poets and critics, most justly esteemed authorities, most brilliantly perceptive persons, do not unflaggingly maintain a very much higher level than these undergraduates. I take my examples at random with a feeling that choice is invidious and a firm opinion that equally good examples will be found in any expository work which comes sufficiently near its subject matter to run any risks. If I begin with Coleridge, I shall not be suspected of intending any disparagement of the authors I cite from:

It is a well-known fact, that bright colours in motion both make and leave the strongest impressions on the eye. Nothing is more likely too, than that a vivid image or visual spectrum, thus originated, may become the link of association in recalling the feelings and images that had accompanied the original impression. But if we describe this in such lines, as

> They flash upon the inward eye,
> Which is the bliss of solitude!

in what words shall we describe the joy of retrospection, when the images and virtuous actions of a whole well-spent life, pass before that conscience which is indeed the *inward* eye: which is indeed '*the bliss of solitude*'? (*Biographia Literaria*, Chapter XXII. It is worth remarking that of Coleridge's three examples of Wordsworth's '*mental* bombast', this and the third show an equally wilful twist in the interpretation and that the second, from *The Gypsies*, is hardly by Coleridge's own showing an example of *excess* of thought to the circumstance and the occasion. I discuss these unhappy noddings further in *Coleridge on Imagination*.)

Professor Garrod on the *Ode to Psyche* may follow:

Keats will be the priest of Psyche, priest and choir and shrine and grove; she shall have a fane 'in some untrodden region of the mind', and shall enjoy.

> all soft delight
> That shadowy thought shall win.

There shall be a 'bright torch' burning for her, and the casement shall be open to let her in at night. I do not find that any commentator has seized the significance of this symbolism. The open window and the lighted torch—they are to admit and attract the timorous *moth-goddess*, who symbolizes melancholy love. (*Keats*, p. 98.)

If it were not Psyche but Cupid, 'the warm Love', who is

to be let in, the slowness of the commentators would not be surprising.

An example from Rupert Brooke will round off this little collection. After pointing out that Webster's

> So perfect shall be thy happiness, that, as men at sea think land and trees and ships go that way they go, so both heaven and earth shall seem to go your journey

was derived from Montaigne:

> As they who travel by sea, to whom mountains, fields, towns, heaven and earth, seem to go the same motion, and keep the same course they do

he adds a footnote: 'Note, though, that Montaigne has made a slip. They really appear to be moving in the *opposite* direction to yourself. Webster takes the idea over, mistake and all.' Those who are not clear, in this case, as to who was mistaken may try the experiment of watching *distant* objects on their next railway journey.

I may now, under the shelter of these examples, offer a paraphrase exposition of my own for the Landor passage, a venture—after so many shipwrecks surveyed—calling for some resolution.

> Young, eager, idle, active, irresponsible (*panting*, further, has a very large number of metaphoric implications—it is a typical 'wheel' metaphor, the spokes being different relations to a more or less connected rim), made thirsty, heated, needing rest, refreshment (with some others of the symbolic senses of water); I read Shakespeare and underwent the influences which lead a man to write and read poetry. *Too* can here couple almost any of the sense items: I, like Shakespeare; I, like others; Avon as well as other influences; Shakespeare as well . . . *Drank of Avon* is a 'wheel within wheel' metaphor, revolving, in one set of motions, together with *panting* and, in another set of motions, together with *dangerous draught* and *feverish thirst*. The influence is thirst-arousing, perhaps salt, intoxicant, alternative. (These motions bring in a very mixed and fleeting throng of feelings.)
> Yet it is impossible, not allowed (feeling of injustice suffered, or of regret alone, as the emphasis is moved from *I* back to *never*)

to me—whatever my merits (in a matter where 'even a little seems a lot' and 'the greatest is unworthy')—to

1. Perform the 'Orphic' functions of the Poet.
2. Write in the spirit or purpose or manner, and on the subjects, of Homer, Virgil, Dante, Shakespeare.

The specific form of the metaphor here loads the statement with feelings of loss and inevitability—the vanishing of a possibility of the mind.

An act in human history is over, it comes to an end like a day. What was known in it—the distances and heights, the symbols of man's strength and security, his hope and religion—cannot be recaptured (as symbols, *hills, turrets,* and *spires,* like the suggested water of line two, have powers upon feeling independent of any specific interpretations that may be stressed by individual readers, they carry a general feeling for which any detailed exposition would be chiefly a rationalization). Can any poet now restore *those* powers of poetry (Apollo, Animism, Belief) that are themselves now closing a cycle?

The exercise of penning such a set of indications brings out, much better than any reading, the kind of elusiveness such meanings enjoy. The mental process—the developing understanding—is what we need to catch, and the words of an account are suited chiefly to the catching of parts of the product. They artificially precipitate much that in the normal reading of the poem remains in solution—but not therefore, if invisible, inactive. This explains some of the oddities in the accounts. The reader who is experimenting with alternative formulations has already, in the words of the poem, a better set of signs than he—being ordinarily no very good poet—is likely to be able to contrive. And he cannot, in the present state of this subject, take the other course and write as a man of science. What he gives us will not, as a rule, state anything that he has found and we must not read him—though the temptation is persistent and strong—as though his sentences were statements. As such they would often be absurd; as signs, though inadequate, they may show us something of what has been happening.

'Poetry gives most pleasure when only generally not perfectly understood.' 'Perfect' understanding might here be a product, something which a sufficiently delicate and elaborate account might represent, an end-state of thought and feeling to which understanding had led. It would obviously be possible to make up a rough scale with specimens of poetry arranged according to the degree to which their meanings settled down finally and remained fixed. We might then find that this scale agreed often with our usual rankings. Some would find this so, others not.

Whether this were so or not, one moral of immense critical importance emerges undeniably from any close study of the process of interpretation, of understanding, of reading. Like most critical morals it is hardly a novelty, though its observance would have novel results. It is this, that a judgment seemingly about a poem is primarily evidence about a reading of it. There are ways of reading almost any poem so as to make it magnificent or ludicrous. Opinions about it to either effect really tell us how it has been read. Every critical opinion is an ellipsis; a conditional assertion with the conditional part omitted. Fully expanded it would state that if a mind of a certain sort, under certain conditions (stage of its development, width of its recoverable experience, height of its temporary vigilance, direction of its temporary interest, etc.), has, at scores, or hundreds, or thousands of points in the growth of its response to certain words, taken certain courses; then such and such. But, as a rule, it seems to be immediately about a certain fictional public object, a projected experience, the poem. It pretends to be, and is usually taken to be, a categoric assertion, discussible as though it were in simple logical relations, of agreement or contradiction and so on, with other assertions of the same type. But these also are collapsed conditional statements. Marvellously alike though we are, it would be fantastic to suggest that our interpretations are often sufficiently similar for critical discussions to yield *the kind of profit we profess to expect*. But they may yield a different profit in increased knowledge of, and skill with, ourselves and others.

It may seem that on this view the difference between good and bad reading has gone; that there is no sense left for 'correct' as applied to interpretations. This would be a mistake. We can always give a sense to a word if we want one, and here we more than want, we *need* a sense for 'correct', or rather, we need several. One for occasions when we are asking about communication, another for semantics, another for orthology, another for general critical purposes, and yet another for the comparison of readings. To take this last only, the *tests*, we should ordinarily say, for the correctness of any interpretation of a set of complex signs are its internal coherence and its coherence with all else that is relevant. But this is an unnecessarily fictitious way of talking. We can say instead that this inner and outer coherence is the correctness. When an interpretation hangs together (without conflicting with anything else: history, literary tradition, etc.) we call it correct—when it takes into account all the items given for interpretation and orders the other items, by which it interprets them, in the most acceptable manner. There are problems behind such a formulation. Correct interpretations of bad and good writing will not hang together in the same specific ways, for example, but though these problems are large ones there seems nothing to prevent an inquiry which would be repaying. We may not have 'the correct interpretation' of a passage and we probably wont have it and we might not recognize it for such if we had it; in this our definition agrees nicely with the ordinary use of 'correct'—which perhaps follows some such definition as 'corresponding' to what was in 'the poet's mind'. But ours has this advantage, that we need not, in judging correctness, attempt, even by fiction, to trespass across Acheron.

The reader may be glad to have the opening three lines of *Gebir*, III—omitted by me in this experiment to heighten the difficulty:

> O for the spirit of that matchless man
> Whom nature led throughout her whole domain,
> While he, embodied, breath'd etherial air.

I do not think that their presence would have made much difference to the comments.

XVIII

Troilus and Cressida and Plato[1]

'IN *Troilus*, all Chaucer's characters are debased, even
Pandarus, hard as the task may seem. Cressida is a
wily profligate, Troilus a whining babbler.' This judgment from Jusserand[2] may serve us as an excellent warning against reading the views of our own day into Shakespeare. We are a long way now from Jusserand, but
equally exposed to this danger—and more exposed to the
worse risk of supposing that the meanings we may rightly
find in the work are to be limited by what we can conjecture to have been Shakespeare's intentions. These Notes,
on what *Troilus and Cressida* may say to readers who have
recently gained an acquaintance with the *Iliad* and the
Republic (in a General Education programme, for example), try to dodge between these dangers. Shakespeare's
works are the offspring of Language and Tradition—of
English in a peculiarly inflamed state and of a meander
of the tradition which proved to be more than ordinarily
fertile. We may reasonably find meanings in the plays
without attributing them to Shakespeare himself; remembering that we have to find them and not plant them there
ourselves.

Jusserand will remind us of another danger—the conventional wrenching of the detached line. 'Even in his

---

[1] Reprinted from *The Hudson Review*, Fall, 1948
[2] *A Literary History of the English People*, Vol. III, p. 253.

most hastily composed plays . . . just as we were about to revolt, to protest against a puppet show, behold, the magician emerges from his torpor, life circulates, and the wooden doll of a moment ago now utters words that no ages can ever forget.'[1] In a footnote: 'Example: to Ulysses, a mere puppet through most of the play, is given the famous line: "One touch of nature makes the whole world kin" (*Troilus*, III, iii, 181).' This is indeed a famous line. In spite of many protests, it will continue to be quoted as if the 'one touch of nature' were something like 'one impulse from the vernal wood' and not an ignoble slavery to fashion:

> That all with one consent praise new borne gaudes.

More lessons lie here than can be enumerated. We have to try to take them to heart.

In this case both the fame and the wrenching seem more than usually explicable. In moods of general benevolence, to think of the whole world becoming kin is agreeable and relieves anxiety. And it seems particularly appropriate that this should happen through 'one touch of nature', as though nature were some sweet recreative influence restoring us to an original innocence. The *kin-kind* pun becomes active perhaps. In contrast, the specifying line is unflattering, painfully true, pointing to things that good-hearted folk would rather not think of. Worse still, *this* 'touch of nature', which unites us in such a humbling bond, seems (if we stress '*one* touch' as I think we should) to be set over against other touches of nature apt to seal us all up 'in will peculiar and self-admission'.

These estimates of *Troilus and Cressida* and of its characters seem to be still widely received. I have heard highly accredited opinion voice a doubt whether the play deserves a place in a General Education course even as a sequence to Homer and Plato. I hope here to give some reasons for

[1] *Op. cit.*, p. 310.

thinking that conventional views underestimate the play;
that its scenes are among the most summoning of Shakespeare's glances at life, that they have at least an affinity
with and an elective power of reflecting Plato at his height;
in particular that Troilus is as little a 'whining babbler'
as Ulysses is a 'wooden doll', and in general that current
interpretations misread the play as badly as the tag-
quotation mistakes the famous line.

Our conception of Troilus himself will, of course, be
the key to the rest of the argument. But since Ulysses is
the source of a major piece of testimony about Troilus we
may well consider the Prince of Ithaca a moment. His
great speech on order (I, iii, 75–137) has received de-
served attention. Less has been paid to his aspect as head
of an Intelligence Service. As he himself claims to
Achilles (III, iii, 202):

> There is a mystery—with whom relation
> Durst never meddle—in the soul of state . . .
> All the commerce that you have had with Troy
> As perfectly is ours as yours, my lord.

In this mystery Ulysses is a master. He proves it at
point after point in the play—with Achilles throughout,
with Ajax (II, iii, 101) , with Cressida (IV, v, 54–63),
with the movements of Diomede (IV, v, 278–82; V, i, 93)
and all through Act V, Scene ii. He is the supremely well
qualified man to describe Troilus to Agamemnon:

> The youngest son of Priam, a true knight;
> Not yet mature, yet matchless; firm of word,
> Speaking in deeds and deedless in his tongue;
> Not soon provok'd nor, being provok'd, soon calm'd:
> His heart and hand both open and both free;
> For what he has he gives, what thinks he shows;
> Yet gives he not till judgment guide his bounty,
> Nor dignifies an impare thought with breath:
> Manly as Hector, but more dangerous;
> For Hector, in his blaze of wrath, subscribes
> To tender objects; but he, in heat of action

> Is more vindicative than jealous love.
> They call him Troilus; and on him erect
> A second hope, as fairly built as Hector.
> Thus says Aeneas; one that knows the youth
> Even to his inches, and with private soul
> Did in great Ilion thus translate him to me.

Shakespeare might almost have had Jusserand's opinion —'a whining babbler'—in mind when he wrote these lines. Unless there is evidence in Troilus' actual behaviour and speeches that Ulysses is utterly wrong here, we should not set such testimony aside. And when we remember that Shakespeare, here, as so often, is following his sources closely, there is the less reason for minimizing its weight.

Let us look then at what Troilus does and says. In the first scene, he indulges in some most elegant rhetorical sighs. That he blames himself for his passion it would be unfair to use against him; but it may be admitted that these early scenes do little to prepare for what is coming. They do not point forward to philosophic action. With the Trojan War Council (II, ii), however, his stature is changed. He becomes the reflective apologist of Honour, a theme and cause (Homeric with a difference) in which he easily triumphs over Helenus:

> You are for dreams and slumbers, brother priest,
> You fur your gloves with reasons

and even over Hector himself, who at the end cries out:

> I am yours,
> You valiant offspring of great Priamus.

The argument of this scene is the mainspring of the play and will, I believe, repay as much examination as any reader has time to give to it. In line 53 comes Troilus' great question—which Act V, Scene ii is to force him to rethink:

> What is aught but as 'tis valued?

Hector's answer can be read, I suggest, with profit, as a comment on Troilus' own later struggle with this truly central problem of all philosophy: value and fact, the ideal and the actual, or however we care to phrase it.

> But value dwells not in particular will;
> It holds his estimate and dignity
> As well wherein 'tis precious of itself
> As in the prizer. 'Tis mad idolatry
> To make the service greater than the god;
> And the will dotes, that is inclinable
> To what infectiously itself affects,
> Without some image of the affected merit.

Each sentence here and every word (especially the small ones, the *as well*, the *of itself*, and the *in*) deserves the fullest imaginative study. Troilus is to face his own 'mad idolatry', to measure the service with the god in the instance of Cressida—driven to it by the sharpest case of jilting in literature—and, above all, to watch the division and reunion of will and reason in himself under the severest testing that they can perhaps be given. He has a long way to go before this and here he replies to Hector chiefly in terms of fidelity—with a marriage figure:

> How may I avoid,
> Although my will distaste what it elected,
> The wife I chose? There can be no evasion
> To blench from this and to stand firm by honour.

He is not announcing his marriage (see IV, ii, 73); he is simply using the image most present to his mind. In his next speech, the lines:

> We may not think the justness of each act
> Such and no other than event doth form it,

are again premonitory and perhaps exculpative.

Hector praises these speeches but quotes Aristotle's echo of the *Republic* (539) and finds them superficial. He then in the spirit of Plato's great analogy (matrimony apart) parallels the individual will with that of the state:

> Nature craves
> All dues be render'd to their owners . . .
> If this law
> Of Nature be corrupted through affection

(a pivotal word in the play)

> And that great minds, of partial indulgence
> To their benumbed wills, resist the same,
> There is a law in each well-order'd nation
> To curb those raging appetites that are
> Most disobedient and refractory.

Then suddenly, in spite of 'these moral laws of nature and of notions' and though

> Hector's opinion
> Is this, in way of truth,

he veers. With an infirmity of purpose which supports Ulysses' judgment of him and with a feckless gallantry matching the poor strategy of his 'roisting challenge' (l. 208), he joins Paris and Troilus:

> My sprightly brethren, I propend to you
> In resolution to keep Helen still;
> For 'tis a cause that hath no mean dependance
> Upon our joint and several dignities.

The contrast between this inconsequence and the policies of 'that same dog-fox Ulysses' is one of many which make the play an exercise in meditation on the sources of power.

The Orchard scene (III, ii) shows us a Troilus in whom I see no ground to doubt his own description:

> I am as true as truth's simplicity
> And simpler than the infancy of truth.

Truth, as he sees it, is indeed in its infancy here. It is to grow up swiftly. That he prefaces these lines with an 'Alas!' and something very like a determination to be deaf to certain doubts about Cressida, does not in the least impair them.

How we see Troilus here depends in a measure upon how we conceive Cressida. I like to make her very young —almost with her little finger hooked in her mouth still —an actress through and through, trying out her powers without caring or knowing much about the roles she picks up or drops. Something of this sort fits both the giddy speed of her transitions (rather than betrayals) and these queer forebodings in Troilus both here and in the farewell scene at dawn. Poor Cressida. Truly she has

> an unkind self, that itself will leave,
> To be another's fool . . .
>   I know not what I speak.

To such a natural putter-on of possible passions Shakespeare can give language of great power:

> Time, force and death,
> Do to this body what extremes you can;
> But the strong base and building of my love
> Is as the very centre of the earth,
> Drawing all things to it. (IV, ii, 108.)

Troilus (III, ii, 186) simply said, 'as earth to the centre'. This young novice Cressida is an experimentalist in feelings, curious and sparing as a wine taster, though exuberant in expression:

> PANDARUS. Be moderate, be moderate.
> CRESSIDA. Why tell you me of moderation?
> The grief is fine, full, perfect, that I taste,
> And violenteth in a sense as strong
> As that which causeth it: how can I moderate it?
> If I could temporize with my affection . . . (IV, iv, 1–6.)

Neither Cressida, nor Troilus in his following speech, know what they are saying. Only the audience—or the close re-reader with the whole play in mind—can see what is happening or into what examples their words will turn them. The fashion in which Cressida can temporize (intemperately) with her affection will be Troilus' punishment for the words he now utters. With Arachne and

Niobe coming later in the play (and in Troilus' own
mouth) it is hard to suppose that the ensuing specimen of
hubris is accidental. 'What a pair of spectacles is here!' as
Pandarus cries, with more reason than he knows. (I must
in passing protest against the traditional excess of contempt[1] for this tender-hearted and fanciful snob. He has
laid aside, it is true, the oath-breaking bow of the *Iliad* to
play Cupid. He has, no doubt in a superior degree, the
vicarious eroticism of the matchmaker, but the insult I
have quoted from Jusserand is unfair to Chaucer and to
Shakespeare as well as to Pandar. It is letting his name
take over the offices of perception and judgment.) 'How
now, lambs!' he says.

> TROILUS. Cressid, I love thee in so strain'd a purity,
> That the bless'd gods, as angry with my fancy,
> More bright in zeal than the devotion which
> Cold lips blow to their deities, take thee from me.
> CRESSIDA. Have the gods envy?
> PANDARUS. Ay, ay, ay, ay; 'Tis too plain a case.

It is truly. And for this blasphemy they *will* take his god-
dess from him, farther than to the Greek camp.

> TROILUS. Hark! you are call'd: some say the Genius so
> Cries 'Come!' to him that instantly must die.

This Genius, however he got here, comes from the
Republic: 'And Lachesis sent with each, as the guardian of
his life and the fulfiller of his choice, the genius that he
he had chosen' (X, 620E). Its business is to see that we
do not escape the life-plan we have selected from among
those cast before us. It is the same Being which Shakespeare put into *Julius Caesar*, II, i, 63–69:

> BRUTUS. Between the acting of a dreadful thing
> And the first motion, all the interim is
> Like a phantasma or a hideous dream:

[1] '. . . The filthy, prurient, self-appointed tool, who revels in garbage
of words and garbage of deeds . . .': The Arden Shakespeare, 1906. *The
Interpretation of Dreams* came into English in 1913.

The genius and the mortal instruments
Are then in council, and the state of man,
Like to a little kingdom, suffers then
The nature of an insurrection.

These lines share two things with *Troilus and Cressida*: this
Genius, so unlike the others in Shakespeare; and the image
of the state of man in insurrection, also derived, ultimately, from the *Republic*:[1]

Kingdom'd Achilles in commotion rages
And batters down himself. (II, iii, 186–8.)

We will pass now to the Betrayal Scene (V, ii) where
the strength of the government in Troilus is tested. With
Ulysses at his elbow and Thersites (another sort of con-
noisseur in human nature) suitably prone in the other
wing as observers and chorus, Troilus has to watch
Cressida, at the mouth of Calchas' tent, *palter* (it is
Diomede's word) with her new lover. He has to see the
sleeve he gave to her as a love-token, 'five-finger-tied' (I
think) to Diomede's helmet.

Before considering the crisis speeches, it is well to consider what sort of shock Troilus is undergoing:

ULYSSES. You shake, my lord, at something: will you go?
You will break out.

and with what measures he is attempting to meet it:

TROILUS. She strokes his cheek!
ULYSSES.   Come, come.
TROILUS. Nay, stay; by Jove, I will not speak a word:
There is between my will and all offences
A guard of patience.

As Cressida goes to fetch the sleeve, Ulysses, with his
hand—thought-readerwise—on Troilus' shoulder, says:

You have sworn patience.
TROILUS.   Fear me not, sweet lord.
I will not be myself, nor have cognition
Of what I feel: I am all patience.

[1] I have written elsewhere, in *How To Read a Page* (p. 74) of the
Platonic echoes in I, iii, 116–24.

Such unnatural self-control cannot last. This guard of patience, though reinforced, as it is, *seven* times in the Scene (whether through the Language or the Tradition, does it not come from the *Republic*?) cannot be expected to hold down for ever a city in such turmoil.

> Never did young man fancy
> With so eternal and so fixed a soul.

It is 'as true as Troilus'; and this man, as we know from Ulysses,

> in heat of action
> Is more vindicative than jealous love.

Something has to happen. We have to consider, as we watch it happening, what it is, and by what canons this behaviour is exemplary.

SOCRATES: Poetry copies men: acting either under force or of their own free will; seeing themselves in the outcome to have done well or ill; and, in all this, feeling grief or joy. Is there something in addition?

GLAUCON: Nothing.

SOCRATES: Is a man of one mind with himself in all this? Or is there division and fighting with himself—as there was when in vision he had opposite opinions at the same time about the same things. . . . Our souls at any one time are attacked by endless opposite views. There was one thing, however, we didn't say then which has to be said now . . . A good man who is ruled by reason will take such blows of fate as the loss of a son or anything very dear to him less hardly than other people. . . . So, because there are two opposite impulses in such a man at the same time about the same thing, we say there are two things in him. One of them is ready to be guided by the law which, I take it, says that it is best to keep quiet as far as possible when griefs come and not to cry out, because we are not certain what is good and what is evil in such things, and to take them hardly does not make them any better. Reason says that nothing in man's existence is to be taken so seriously, and our grief keeps us back from the very thing we need as quickly as possible in such times.

GLAUCON: What is that?

SOCRATES: To take thought on the event; and, as we order our play by the way the cards fall, to see how to order our acts, in view of what has come about, in the ways reason points to as the best. Don't let us be like children when they have had a fall, and go on crying out with a hand on the place. Look after the wound first and pick up what has had a fall, and make grief give place to medical help. (*Republic*, 603–4.)

Or consider again:

SOCRATES: And don't the best things undergo the least changes and motions that come to them from other things . . . For example, the body is changed by meat and drink and work, and every plant by the light of the sun and the wind. . . . But isn't the change least in the plant or body that is healthiest and strongest? So of the soul. It will be the bravest and wisest soul which is least moved and changed from without. (*Republic*, 381.)

Again, it may be through Language or Tradition (and we may separate or combine these with the greatest of ease) that the conception of the self-governing soul controls this scene. Now we watch it meeting a storm which could readily break the heart or overthrow the reason of a less healthy or weaker being than Troilus.

ULYSSES. All's done my lord.
TROILUS. It is.
ULYSSES. Why stay we, then?
TROILUS. To make a recordation to my soul
Of every syllable that here was spoke.

His impulse to disbelieve is going to make him forget what he has seen and heard—unless he forestalls it—much as Darwin is said to have made *immediate* note of discrepant facts. By the next line but one:

Shall I not lie in publishing a truth?

the cleavage is beginning. The old faith and hope, and new evidence and despair, are too strong for one another:

Sith yet there is a credence in my heart
An esperance so obstinately strong,
That doth invert the attest of eyes and ears
As if those organs had deceptious functions,
Created only to calumniate.

Something has to give way; who was it at the mouth of Calchas' tent?

TROILUS. Was Cressid here?
ULYSSES.   I cannot conjure, Trojan.
TROILUS. She was not, sure.
ULYSSES.   Most sure she was.
TROILUS. Why, my negation hath no taste of madness.

He carries this far enough to make Thersites wonder: 'Will he swagger himself out on's own eyes?' But the two truths are so equal that this is no way out. Something must break and it is Cressid who divides:

> this is, and is not, Cressid.

'What is aught but as 'tis valued?' When the valuations become irreconcilable and insuperable, the thing splits and the thinker (or thinger) then has to remain *one* (if he can) himself:

TROILUS. This she? no, this is Diomede's Cressida.
If beauty have a soul, this is not she,

(That which he loved in her, was not this)

If souls guide vows, if vows are sanctimony,

(Two certainties, if *vows* and *sanctimony* are understood aright)

If sanctimony be the gods' delight,

(SOCRATES: Do the gods love sanctimony because it is sanctimony? Or is it sanctimony because the gods love it? ... What is this art of serving the gods, Euthyphro? What the great result of it? The care of the soul?)

If there be rule in unity itself,
This is not she.

(The very thing which holds him together and keeps the universe from shaking to pieces must make this separation in her)

> O madness of discourse,
> That cause sets up, with and against itself,
> Bi-fold authority!

(In this consists a spirit, that it is self-reflective.)

The two in Troilus that correspond to the two Cressids change place: reason, the very rule in unity itself, safely throwing off its own authority, and that very perdition (which is also loss of one of the Cressids) taking up the rule:

> where reason can revolt
> Without perdition, and loss assume all reason
> Without revolt.

This is language become itself a translucent instance of what it would describe; it both *says* what it means and illustrates it. Troilus, absorbed now in the mystery of how

> this is and is not Cressid,

seems to draw from the stroke itself the resolution. The opposites are all before him

> more wider than the sky and earth

and yet they come together and are indistinguishable—as Ariadne's clue and Arachne's web are merged in 'Ariachne's broken woof'. (An escape from a labyrinth containing a devouring monster, with an ensuing betrayal; a penalty for *hubris* with a horrible transformation.) With that *broken*, however anguishingly it echoes, we know that it applies not to his heart but to whatever held him to Cressid—some fabric of gossamer texture. And as the last waves of this earthquake subside we can compare the hard darkness of:

> strong as Pluto's gates

with an airy brightness:

> strong as heaven itself

and feel the expansion and reunion occurring already in this suddenly restored lover. The bonds of heaven, that seemed so strong, are dissolv'd. We see through Troilus' eyes what it is that

> with another knot, five-finger-tied

Diomede has gained:

> orts of her love
> The fragments scraps, the bits and greasy reliques
> Of her o'er-eaten faith.

And discerning Ulysses here speaks for us when he asks,

> May worthy Troilus be half attach'd
> With that which here his passion doth express?

Troilus' reply shows us that he knows how to deal with that half-attachment. In Coleridge's words, 'having a depth of calmer element in a will stronger than desire, more entire than choice . . . the same moral energy is represented as snatching him aloof from all neighbour-hood with her dishonour.' It is like Shakespeare to give the summing-up to his almost monstrously detached and avid observer, the sick artist.

THERSITES. He'll tickle it for his concupy.

When Aeneas arrives seeking him, this 'whining babbler' is almost whole again.

TROILUS. Have with you, prince. My courteous lord, adieu.
Farewell, revolted fair! and, Diomede,
Stand fast, and wear a castle on thy head.
ULYSSES. I'll bring you to the gates.
TROILUS. Accept distracted thanks.

*　　*　　*

TROILUS. The bless'd gods as angry with my fancy
. . . take thee from me.
CRESSIDA. Have the gods envy?
TROILUS. If sanctimony be the god's delight . . .
This is not she.

Socrates, in puzzling Euthyphro—a very Deuterono-
mic sort of young man—with questions about the service
and the god and the outcome of the service, is keeping well
within that self-confident theologian's intellectual reach,
almost within his grasp. But Plato was to give Socrates
other questions which were to empty such inquiries as:

If sanctimony be the god's delight.

In the more than sunlight of the Idea of the Good, 'which
gives true being to whatever deep knowledge is of, and
the power of knowing to the knower' (*Republic*, 508), all
contrasts between the things the gods value and their
valuings fade out. 'What is aught but as 'tis valued?' is a
dangerous question, as Hector pointed out, when applied
to 'particular will'. But it is other words for the Idea of
the Good if the valuing is that of knowledge. And 'Have
the gods envy?'—which Homer's Achilles could ask as
literally as any child—turns, on reflection, into a deep
inquiry about

> degree, priority and place,
> Insisture, course, proportion, season, form,
> Office, and custom, in all line of order. (I, iii, 86–9.)

Troilus does misplace his adoration. And to do that *is* to
offend the jealous gods. Indeed the more closely we read
the two Council Scenes, the more closely knit

If there be rule in unity itself,

this 'most hastily composed play' will be found. Even in
what may seem no more than Agamemnon's preliminary
remarks:

> which are indeed naught else
> But the protractive trials of great Jove,
> To find persistive constancy in men

even in these

> there is seen
> The baby figure of the giant mass
> Of things to come at large.

This is not unusual in Shakespeare—though this play, with *Julius Caesar*, is unwontedly thick with premonitions and echoes. What is exceptional, to my mind, is the degree to which its central thought seems to accord with Plato's. Others have wondered whether 'the strange fellow' who had written to Ulysses (III, iii, 95) might not have been Plato. I find a strange fellowship throughout. And perhaps the strangeness is the condition of the fellowship:

> For speculation turns not to itself
> Till it hath travell'd, and is married there
> Where it may see itself.

Index